A LITTLE GUIDE TO
CHRI
SPIRIT

A LITTLE GUIDE TO

CHRISTIAN SPIRITUALITY

THREE

DIMENSIONS

OF LIFE

WITH GOD

With every good wish in Christ,

GLEN G. SCORGIE

ZONDERVAN®

ZONDERVAN.com/
AUTHORTRACKER
follow your favorite authors

A Little Guide to Christian Spirituality
Copyright © 2007 by Glen G. Scorgie

Requests for information should be addressed to:
Zondervan, *Grand Rapids, Michigan* 49530

Library of Congress Cataloging-in-Publication Data

Scorgie, Glen G.
    A little guide to christian spirituality: three dimensions of life with God /
Glen G. Scorgie.
       p. cm.
    Includes bibliographical references.
    ISBN-10: 0-310-27459-1
    ISBN-13: 978-0-310-27459-9
    1. Spirituality. 2. Spiritual life — Christianity. I. Title.
BV4501.3.S39 2007
248.4 — dc22
2006102160

Interior design by Michelle Espinoza

Printed in the United States of America

---

08 09 10 11 12 • 23 22 21 20 19 18 17 16 15 14 13 12 11 10 9 8 7 6 5 4 3 2

To the memory of Lilyan Alberta Scorgie—
mother, mentor, and woman of God

ALSO BY GLEN G. SCORGIE

A Call for Continuity
The Challenge of Biblical Translation (coeditor)
The Journey Back to Eden

CONTENTS

Prologue: Sleeping through A. W. Tozer's Last Sermon / 9

Introduction: Two Saints under One Hood / 15

1. Getting Started / 21

PART 1: THE RELATIONAL DYNAMIC: CHRIST *with* US

2. Friendship with God / 39

3. Experiencing Community / 55

PART 2: THE TRANSFORMATIONAL DYNAMIC: CHRIST *in* US

4. The Renewal of Holiness / 73

5. The Healing of Our Wounds / 87

PART 3: THE VOCATIONAL DYNAMIC: CHRIST *through* US

6. Discovering Purpose and Meaning / 105

7. The Gift of a Personal Calling / 121

8. An Integrated Spirituality / 137

9. Living with Disciplined Intent / 153

Epilogue: Yearning for Better Days / 171

Questions for Individual and Group Reflection / 177

Going Deeper: Resources for Further Study / 181

Notes / 185

SLEEPING THROUGH A. W. TOZER'S LAST SERMON

The roots of this book go back many years, and I will start by acknowledging some of my earliest debts. It was Sunday night in downtown Toronto over forty years ago. The preacher with a narrow mustache moved to the pulpit. He first flexed his bony shoulders, as always, and then started in. Down below I was stretched out on a hard, creaky pew between my mom and dad, and slept right through the sermon. As it turned out, it was the last time the mystic A. W. Tozer ever preached. He went home that night and died soon after.

Later on I got to see his private upstairs study in his narrow little house, where he used to lay face down on the floor to pray and place his nose on a handkerchief to protect his lungs from rug dust. I treasure the memory of a man who once loaned me one of his big picture books of birds—cardinals in bold red, exquisite little bluebirds, Baltimore orioles flaunting their orange and black to the glory of God, and stunning yellow goldfinches—an extravagance of color, and a fascination the great man and a little boy happened to share. But ever since that night when I slept through Tozer's last sermon, I've felt a sympathetic kinship to Eutychus.

❧

Winter was approaching Saskatchewan, with gauzelike skiffs of snow blowing across the one paved highway in and out of our little town Outlook. The Reverend Hobson, an Englishman with a charming accent and a wife who could sing, had come to hold a week of special meetings at our church, probably feeling as if he had arrived at the end of the earth. He was an associate of Major Ian Thomas, promulgating the Keswick teaching on the so-called "deeper Christian life." Only a scattering of people showed up to hear him speak. Yet through his influence that week I came into a freeing and empowering experience of consecration. And while that particular stream of spirituality left me with excruciating questions about the relationship between "the crucifixion of self" and the validity of my personal identity and will, it introduced me to the interior life of intimacy with God.

♪

Every April, when melting snow was filling up the farm dugouts, the birds were back singing after long months of absence, and farmers were lubricating their ramshackle machinery in preparation for seeding, church folk would pack up and head west to Prairie Bible Institute for Spring Conference. Thousands of people—shy, weatherbeaten men, and their wives in homemade dresses—gathered in the Prairie Tabernacle in Three Hills, Alberta for a semiannual fix of soul nourishment. Groups of singers in matching outfits and every conceivable configuration—male, female, mixed, choirs, quintets, quartets, trios, duets, and soloists—lifted the spirits, while special speakers expounded the Word and challenged people to greater commitment to the Great Commission.

At Prairie it was always relatively easy to recruit young people to lifelong overseas missionary service. The fact was, it seems to me, that everyone was so poor already that there was not much they had to give up. To many ardent young folk, Burma or the Belgian Congo sounded more interesting than returning to a marginal farm outside of Moose Jaw or Elbow.

But the real draw at the Spring Conferences was always L. E. Maxwell. He was the founding principal of Prairie Bible Institute—an immigrant from Kansas with some connections to the early Pentecostal phenomena there at the turn of the century. He was so absolutely full of energy and the joy of the Lord that sometimes it seemed as though his wired little body would be unable to contain it. He jumped and shouted and rejoiced around the platform, enthused beyond belief that he was "expendable" and Christ was everything. It was contagious. And you could feel your soul "transported" into some other dimension of insight and certitude as he expounded the Scriptures. I recall being so carried away as a teenager that I actually signed a personal pledge card for missions—agreeing to pay off a faith-stretching sum in monthly installments over the next year.

Later that night, as I lay on my upper bunk in the spartan men's dormitory, I was enveloped in such a sense of well-being that the room seemed radiant. Looking back, from a doctrinal perspective the messages were all stock fundamentalism, but there was some genuine life to it too.[1]

∽

Many years later my wife and I went off to Regent College in Vancouver to study theology and church history, and it felt like I had finally come home. J. I. Packer, James Houston, Ian Rennie, and the late Klaus Bockmuehl embodied a blend of evangelical spirituality and clear-mindedness that made them mentors and models for many of us. An English Anglican, a Scottish Brethren, a Canadian Presbyterian, and a Pietistic German Lutheran—they all widened our horizons. For good reasons Packer has been described as the last of the Puritans. Up close, his orthodoxy is combined with a gentleness, humility, grace, and wit that have always been profoundly winsome.

James Houston, a brilliant Scottish geographer, grew up in the biblically literate but separatist atmosphere of the Christian Brethren. Yet this man, from such an unlikely professional career and church tradition—indeed, God seems to delight in ironies!—pioneered the exploration and recovery for evangelicals of Christianity's historic spiritual resources in their widest, ecumenical scope. Meanwhile he has nurtured countless others with the insights he has harvested. His discernment, gift for mentoring, and uncanny knack for being present when needed, are legendary.

Klaus Bockmuehl modeled the solemn privilege and responsibility of a Christian scholar. On a ferry back and forth between the British Columbia mainland and Vancouver Island one weekend, I recall devouring a little book he had recommended to his class. A. G. Sertillanges's *The Intellectual Life* highlighted the legitimacy, for those called to it, of an academic vocation in the service of Christ. It freed me up to be myself.

And Ian Rennie, a great Canadian church historian and raconteur, somehow managed to draw us, our varied wounds, disillusionments, and horror stories notwithstanding, into his own charitable embrace of the church—warts and all.

୬୧

Closer to the present, I am ever so grateful to Bethel Seminary for sustaining an institutional environment where spirituality is valued and theological research is encouraged. I am especially grateful for a faculty travel grant from the Bethel Alumni Association and for a sabbatical reprieve from teaching duties that enabled me to get a good start on this project. I will always treasure my sabbatical pilgrimages to Iona Abbey in Scotland, various historic sites of spiritual significance in Italy and Turkey, and renewal centers closer to home. I want to thank in particular the *Suore dell'Addolorata* for the extended hospitality at their B and B in Rome, for their inspirational daily chapel singing (in Italian, of course), and for their cheerful ministry to the homeless and unemployed there.

It is such a blessing when a marriage grows into a spiritual friendship. My biggest debt of gratitude, as always, is to amazing Kate—my soul mate through the years.

I am also indebted to those who provided constructive feedback to earlier presentations of this material. My benefactors include the eight members of our graduate seminar on the theology of spirituality and prayer, offered at Bethel Seminary San Diego in 2005. They also include friends at the Chinese Bible Church of San Diego who attended an eight-week series of lectures on this topic there; members of Glory Christian Church and Chinese Evangelical Church of San Diego in southern California retreat settings; another special group at Hillside Baptist Church in Penang; and later on, the faculty and student body of the Malaysia Baptist Theological Seminary, a class of graduate students at the Biblical Seminary of the Philippines in Manila, a group of Chinese pastors in Kota Kinabalu, and the tribal students at the Malaysia Evangelical College in Miri, Borneo.

Finally, I wish to acknowledge those resilient believers who, amid persistent discrimination and opposition, live for Christ and so graciously engaged this material in Bandar Seri Begawan, the capital of the southeast Asian kingdom of Brunei.

I have taken to heart the encouragement and constructive suggestions of all these friends. This little book is better for their input, while the remaining flaws are entirely my responsibility. On this side of eternity, as the apostle Paul acknowledged, at best we know in part (1 Corinthians 13:12).

TWO SAINTS UNDER ONE HOOD

I will pray with my spirit, but I will also pray with my understanding.

1 Corinthians 14:15

It's a damp, lonely business being a graduate student in Scotland. Yet for me it was also a marvelous life highlight. The gray, brooding climate is good thinking weather, and the isolation helps keep distractions at bay. And walking everywhere keeps the mind clear. The most exquisite place in the whole country is St. Andrews, a medieval town built of stone on the coast of the North Sea. Never mind that it is also the home of golf. The ancient town walls are still visible, along with the ruins of a castle once besieged by the French navy and the remains of a once-great oversized cathedral. You can casually park your bicycle over places marked in the cobblestones where ardent young Reformers burned at the stake in the tough early years of the Scottish Reformation. History cozies up close.

St. Mary's College, the divinity school of the University of St. Andrews, has been in operation since 1453. Periodically the robed faculty hosted little gatherings for the graduate students at St. Mary's, and we would be invited into a normally off-limits hall for sherry, cheese, and chitchat. With uncharacteristic extravagance, the tall-ceiling room would be very briefly *heated* for the occasion. We were always eager for some social contact, not to mention an opportunity to dry off, warm up, and enjoy free food.

Standing near the refreshment platter one evening, my attention was drawn to a series of dark oil paintings in large, ostentatious frames along the walls: portraits of former principals of St. Mary's, going back through the centuries. My eyes came to rest on the one of Samuel Rutherford, a seventeenth-century divine and one of Scotland's greatest-ever theologians, political theorists, and devotional writers. He embodied the very best of the Puritan heart and mind.

Through the centuries the Catholic Church has produced numerous orders: voluntary organizations of committed members, usually monks, with distinctive strengths and particular visions for ministry. The Franciscans, founded by Francis of Assisi, were known for their simple faith and personal piety. The Dominicans, an order of preachers and theologians, claimed Thomas Aquinas, *the* theological genius of the Middle Ages, as their most celebrated member. And most members of these orders wore robes, with cowls or hoods to cover their heads in inclement weather.

This brings us back to Rutherford, who managed to combine scholastic learning and mystical piety in a remarkably integrated way. He was, in the words of one writer — and this is what I am setting up — "St. Thomas and St. Francis under one hood." What a wonderful image! Rutherford believed that "the arduous work of academic theology was necessary in order to provide a conceptual framework within which ecstatic spirituality could flourish without spinning into subjectivism."[1] Don't be thrown by the term "ecstatic" — it simply refers to personal religious experience that touches one's heart, feelings, and emotions. And this is exactly what this little book aims to do — to get St. Thomas and St. Francis (so to speak) back together again under one hood.

Spirituality is profoundly popular today. Mainstream bookstore shelves are spilling over with volumes ranging from classic devotionals to the totally bizarre. It is easy to be confused by this cacophony of voices. Quite a few Christians are asking: So what exactly *is* spirituality? And what constitutes a distinctly *Christian* spirituality? As Christians, we need to get a handle on what it's all about. And these are exactly the questions we aim to address in this book.

Beyond these questions, however, another even larger one looms, and it is this: Does the Christian faith *really* have the resources to satisfy this gnawing contemporary hunger? I am convinced that it does. But I am equally convinced that the popular North American *version* of Christianity we have bought into cannot sustain itself over the long haul. This is why I also believe the Holy Spirit is prodding the people of God today to reclaim the rich spiritual resources of our faith and to recover the things that have inspired and sustained believers through the centuries.

Our primary resource in this quest will be the Bible. But the full experience to which the Scriptures point — that is, distinctively Christian spirituality — has been known (to greater or lesser degrees) for almost two thousand years now. The "cloud of witnesses" has left a large legacy of spiritual insight, and this literature continues to accumulate. We are blessed to be so well resourced. But the sheer quantity and diversity of this material can bewilder sincere seekers. We need help to access it with discernment.

This book is not a devotional piece. Rather, it is a little *theology* on an immense subject. Naturally I am not putting it forward as *the* definitive way everyone should view spirituality. I offer it instead as *a* way of seeing, yet one that resonates with Scripture and incorporates important recurring themes in Christian literature, designed for Christians who are prepared to *think* about spirituality as a foundation for practicing it wisely and well.

It is not meant to replace any of the classics, or a single one of the many helpful contemporary treatments of Christian spirituality. Rather, it is offered as a companion to the rest; a navigational guide to orient travelers by providing a basic map of the terrain, some help with local dialects, and a few travel tips along the way. For example, each chapter concludes with brief profiles of "some helpful guides" to deeper understanding and experience.

The mystery of a life lived before God in the power of the Spirit cannot be reduced to a "one size fits all" formula. The Spirit is like the wind, that "blows wherever it pleases. You hear its sound, but you cannot tell where it comes from or where it is going" (John 3:8). No, the best we can do is to identify some pervading themes and recurring emphases. The encouraging thing is that there are some elements that all pilgrims are able instinctively to recognize and affirm as parts of their own experience. The Spirit has his own signature style. He leads us along paths that are similar. Despite the feelings of loneliness that sometimes flood over us, it is comforting to realize that we are not really alone.

There *is* such a thing as a distinctive Christian spirituality, and this book lays out a model for understanding it. It is one that highlights three essential dynamics—three impulses that mix and move together as a single living thing.

Each of the dynamics I describe came to me more or less the hard way—on my own. Only afterward did I become aware that I was not as original as I had thought. Instead, I felt like a person who struggles to blaze a trail upward through the woods to a hilltop, only to discover upon emerging at the peak that other hikers are already there. Other contemporary writers have already structured their thinking around similar triads.[2] When you think about it, this is probably a good sign. Total originality is overrated in such a venerable field as this. After all, we are attempting to describe, in our different ways and from our diverse perspectives, the same reality—the timeless dynamics of the Christian life we share together.

Christian spirituality should be cultivated in dialogue with godly voices from the past *and* present. There is no excuse for ignoring the past, for the kind of attitude C. S. Lewis labeled chronological snobbery. Unfortunately, we tend to sample the literature of spirituality eclectically, and for the most part uncritically. We must do better than to take random biopsies from our spiritual heritage. Such dabbling can lead to imbalances and deficiencies in our understanding and experience.

Our three-dimensional understanding of spirituality helps make sense out of what might otherwise appear a chaotic deluge of devotional information and advice. It *clarifies the goals* toward which the Spirit is moving, and toward which we, then, ought to be intentionally aiming our lives. And it also *provides criteria for evaluating* the strengths and limitations of the various spiritual resources available to us.

In our concluding section, we will note that the three dynamics are interconnected—woven together—and that each is essential to human life as God intended. Not just one or two of them, then, but all three need to be consciously cultivated. The book ends with an invitation to live the Christian life with disciplined intent.

It is tempting to write about Christian spirituality in a partisan way. Certainly there is a place for highlighting the strengths of our respective church traditions and denominations. Even so, the spiritual experience of the people of God is enriched, stimulated, and typically guided back on track by listening to the diverse voices of the larger harmony. It is "together with all the Lord's people" that we are able "to grasp how wide and long and high and deep is the love of Christ" (Ephesians 3:18).

Ultimately we believe there is *one* holy, catholic, and apostolic church—*one* people of God who live and move in his transforming and empowering presence. Beneath our surface idiosyncrasies are the strong, subterranean continuities of our shared life with God. I write as one rooted in the evangelical tradition, but the dynamics of Christian spirituality are known to all those who are embraced by the Father, redeemed by the Son, and open to the Holy Spirit. I invite you to join me now on a journey of discovery. As we set off, let's keep trying to squeeze St. Francis and St. Thomas beneath a single hood. We love God best with heart *and* mind.[3]

GETTING STARTED

The spiritual did not come first, but the natural,
and after that the spiritual.
1 Corinthians 15:46

Years ago our family enjoyed attending a summer Bible conference north of Toronto. It was in the exquisite Muskoka district, nestled between a clear lake and granite ridges covered in pines. The smells of that camp still come to me—bacon grilling in the kitchen, tree gum oozing from rough bark, used oil splashed on gravel roads to keep the dust down, the tuckshop where pop bottles hung in rows in a dark tub of cold water, the canvas walls of a hot tent, gas fumes from an Evinrude outboard motor, and the staring fish we triumphantly carried up from the lake for cleaning.

But I also remember that the motorboats sat idle on Sundays, so we could take meditative walks in the forest and listen to mesmerizing Bible expositors baptize our imaginations in the world of Scripture. A plaque beneath the camp flagpole bore the names of heroic missionary martyrs. And I remember how the loudspeakers, mounted on spindly poles around the grounds, would at 6:00 a.m. sharp begin to crackle with upbeat trumpet music relayed from a record player in the conference office down the hill. On the heels of reveille, a voice would give a cheery wake-up call, inviting one and all to morning prayers. Then, remarkably it seems now, out from the cabins and lodges hidden in the trees, those old saints, already dressed and ready for the day, would begin heading for the chapel. There was a quality of holiness to it all.

The ones who impressed me most were the broken-down missionaries who'd lost their health in prison camps or through repeated bouts of malaria in jungle locations. They took prayer very seriously, fasting too, and spent a lot of their time in the heavenlies. They were spiritual warriors — the real McCoy. Their petitions were global, their personal needs few. And when they turned to us young people and spoke a kindly word or godly admonition, we felt their discerning eyes pierce right through our souls. They spoke of entire consecration in a way that made you feel they really knew what they were talking about. And their ear was always tilted in an attentive way for the still, small voice that guided them. The veil between time and eternity seemed very thin indeed. It seemed a sacred place.

Over time, for financial reasons and the changing demands of Christian guests, the conference's emphasis shifted to more recreation and less spiritual renewal. The buildings were upgraded, and the prices rose. Eventually it was all sold off, and today it is an exclusive sports camp, where rich parents send their kids for summers of parasailing and other elite recreational activities.

As much as I long for those good old days, I am aware that we can never step in the same river twice. We cannot restore some cherished memory. Time moves on. New wine cannot be put in old wineskins. The basic dynamics of authentic Christian spirituality will always be the same, but their forms and expression will be continually new and different. The Spirit is infinitely creative, and we must be open to the fresh and unexpected (though strangely familiar) ways he will graciously meet the next generation.

The Spiritual Yearning of Our Times

There is a great deal of interest in spirituality today. Just about everyone, it seems, is weighing in on the topic, not just the Dalai Lama and the leaders of the other world religions. Hollywood stars, whole food stores, and sports heroes are all into it as well. What's going on?

The explanation lies in a serious shortcoming of modernity—the dominant cultural backdrop to the early twenty-first century. Modernity's defect is that it is hopelessly materialistic. Day after day, from morning to night, our society operates on the assumption that the material world—the world of *stuff*—is all there is. Our world is thought to operate like a self-sustaining machine, according to fixed laws that can be explained by science and manipulated by technology. The notion of an unseen, supernatural dimension beyond this is considered, well, silly. The transcendent, if it exists at all, is of no real concern. Nor is the question of possible life after death. What you see is what you get—period. So enjoy. Indulge. Be happy.

Modernity depicts an absolutely empty universe, stark and friendless beyond the fragile bubble of our planet's atmosphere. It has been skilled at describing what *is*, but is at a loss to propose what *ought* to be. It can offer no point beyond the material horizon by which we aim our lives in straight, purposeful lines. It provides no help beyond what we can create for ourselves.

The older religious worldview depicted a three-story universe, with heaven above and hell beneath. It envisioned a vast expanse of time, from purposeful origins in an intelligent Designer's mind, through responsible existence in the present, to life stretching beyond death to eternity. But modernity has lopped it all away, and collapsed this vast space-time panorama down to the narrow here and now—to movies, cell phones, and protected sex, and seventy to eighty years at the outside.

For some time now, skeptical Western philosophy and relentless materialism have ignored God and squeezed the remaining glimmers of the transcendent out of human experience. Modernity is still seductive, but it is failing to satisfy the soul-hunger of a growing number of people. For our contemporaries the term "spirit" represents what is transcendent, what defies reduction to physical reality. The contemporary quest for "spirituality" is a cry of the human spirit for satisfaction of the deeper needs of creatures with eternity set into their hearts (Ecclesiastes 3:11).

SPIRITUALITY AND ORGANIZED RELIGION

"I consider myself a spiritual person. I'm just not into religion." This is a familiar mantra today. Attitudes toward organized religion have been increasingly negative. People, especially young people, are declaring themselves with their feet. Attendance at church services in America has been in a downward slide for a while now, with no sign of turnaround. Religion is viewed as institutional and diminishing. Spirituality, on the other hand, is thought to transcend dogma, dwell in the region of the heart, and be ultimately empowering. So religion (meaning organized religion) is out and spirituality is in.

Some of this "bad press" for organized religion may be a result of the world's chronic hostility to Jesus Christ and his followers. As the apostle John explained, there is a spirit of falsehood circulating in the world order that predisposes people to react with disdain toward the truth (1 John 4:5 – 6). Jesus Christ himself endured unfair slander, and warned his disciples that they should expect the same (Matthew 10:24 – 25).

But the real question is whether this explanation *fully* accounts for the growing disdain for organized religion, which, in the overwhelming number of cases, means Christian churches. Is it possible that organized religion, if we can borrow the pejorative term for just a moment, has been at least partly responsible for making itself so odious? Let's be honest — is organized religion very effective in facilitating transforming encounter with God? We look back rather wistfully to the first century, when the response of outsiders who visited church was, "God is really among you!" (1 Corinthians 14:25).

Transcendence is atrophying in the contemporary church. Marketing Jesus is intensely demanding. We have time for little else. Our souls are becoming hollowed out. A while back we somehow made the fatal mistake of diving into the world without maintaining any transcendental air hose.[1] And this is where we are. Nothing short of

spiritual renewal of the church will draw those who hunger for God
back into the locus of organized Christianity in the West.

WHAT IS SPIRITUALITY?

Spirituality is "that most slippery of words to pin down."[2] But
we won't get very far here unless we take a moment to think ourselves clear on what we mean by it. One of our three daughters is a
nineteen-year-old literature major who is well connected to pop culture and contemporary values. I get pretty accurate reads on the cur-
rent thought-world by asking her what she thinks. So I questioned her
the other day: "What does spirituality mean to you?" She paused for
a moment and then responded carefully: "It's about encountering the
transcendent and being changed by it."

I think Sarah hit it, as the British say, "spot on." Spirituality in
the generic sense involves an *encounter* with the transcendent (or the
numinous, the Real, or whatever is *ultimately* important), and then
the positive, beneficial *effects* of that encounter on a person. It's about
establishing a transforming connection to something *more*—a connection that will shape who we become and how we will live.

Christians affirm a distinctive version of this definition. Through
the correcting lens of biblical revelation, the "transcendent reality"
of generic spirituality comes into focus as the living, personal triune
God. This is, as we shall see, a gargantuan clarification. And the *effects*
will include growing in Christlikeness and participating in the larger
purposes of God.

CHRISTIAN SPIRITUALITY IS HOLISTIC

Two competing conceptions of spirituality circulate among Christians these days—a narrow one and a holistic one. The narrow version
is concerned with experiencing the presence, voice, and consolations of
God in a direct, right-here-right-now way. It pursues direct encounter
with God's presence—experiences that have been aptly called "eso-
teric moments" and "points of wonder."[3]

Authentic Christianity has always celebrated the possibility of *experiencing* God in this direct and interactive sense. At the same time it has insisted that there is more to being a Christian than this. And this brings us to the holistic definition of spirituality. Such spirituality is about living *all of life* before God. In its full sense spirituality is synonymous with *the Christian life* lived with God. It involves more than experiences, although it has an important place for those. It also encompasses things like repentance, moral renewal, soul-crafting, community building, witness, service, and faithfulness to one's calling.

Evelyn Underhill offers this holistic description: "A spiritual life is simply a life in which all that we do comes from the center, where we are anchored in God: a life soaked through and through by a sense of His reality and claim, and self-given to the great movement of His Will." [4] We should aim for this more holistic understanding of Christian spirituality. But it should be with awareness that enthusiasts for *experiencing* God have put their finger on the weak spot in the dominant brand of religion being offered by institutional Christianity.

SPIRITUALITY AS *Spirit*-UALITY

Everything about Christian spirituality—indeed, everything Christianity has ever had to offer—is grounded in what Jesus Christ has done for us. The eternal Son revealed the face of God. He showed us what God is like. As a human being, he also modeled what we are to become. He gave us a glimpse of our own restored humanity. Not only that—by his life, death and resurrection, and ongoing ministry on our behalf, he makes our own renewal possible. The saving merits and energizing life of Christ now come to us through the Holy Spirit, who is present with us in the world. Presently the Spirit is our point of contact with—indeed, our lifeline to—the triune God.

The roots of the popular word "spirituality" are actually Christian. In the New Testament, the apostle Paul wrote a great deal about the Spirit (*pneuma*) and spiritual persons (*pneumatikoi*). He had something specifically in mind when he did. To Paul's way of thinking, spiritual persons are those who keep in step with the Spirit. The Spirit's role is crucial, for he is the one who mediates the presence, character, and power of the ascended Christ to us. He brings Christ close. So spirituality is about being attentive to the Spirit's voice, open to his transforming impulses, and empowered by his indwelling presence.

The vital connection between the Holy Spirit and Christian spirituality has led New Testament scholar Gordon Fee to offer an intriguing suggestion. As a reminder to ourselves, Christians should consider spelling spirituality with a capital "S" and a hyphen — that is, as *Spirit*-uality.[5] Now we can expand our definition of spirituality a bit further. It is about living all of life before God in the transforming and empowering presence of his Spirit.

THOMAS CAHILL'S CHALLENGE

Not so long ago Thomas Cahill wrote a book entitled *How the Irish Saved Civilization*, a captivating tale of how the Christian faith fared during the first millennium. After its dynamic apostolic launch, Christianity eventually fell under the spell and control of the powerful and administratively gifted Romans. The outcome was the near extinction of the faith and the onset of the Dark Ages. In God's providence, however, Christianity survived and eventually flourished again. Its recovery was not due to the Romans, though, but to the contribution of some obscure but saintly, Spirit-filled Celtic missionaries from Europe's most remote offshore island. History has a way of cycling around again. Cahill concludes his book with this prophetic application to our own time: "The twenty-first century," he says, "will be spiritual or it will not be."[6]

Cahill's remark stimulated my desire to rediscover, if I could, the essential dynamics of Christian spirituality as set forth in Scripture and grasped at the higher points in Christian history. My search started on the little island of Iona, just off the west coast of Scotland, where the Celtic missionaries Cahill talked about had long ago established a significant center for evangelism in pagan territory.

Iona Abbey still stands, and I was determined one night to make it there for a vespers service. It was raining, cold and sideways. The air was full of sharp odors from the sea. The abbey was about a mile from my lodgings in the pitch-black night, and I had forgotten my flashlight. So I groped and stumbled my way past the ruins of a nunnery, along a winding, narrow road, through a little gate, and finally on to the property of the abbey itself. The path before me cut diagonally across the premises and past a cemetery, where converted pagan kings and warlords have lain beneath their tilting Celtic crosses for one and a half millennia.

The path itself was more like a gently molded trench, worn progressively deeper by the feet of centuries. Around the back of the building was a glimmer of light. Following it, I finally pushed into a small stone candlelit room. Over the next few minutes other people found the door and quietly shuffled in. Without words they scraped their heavy wooden chairs across the stone floor as they took seats around the long table and began to shed their rain gear. The room filled with the scent of soaked wool and hot wax.

We celebrated a simple Communion service together. The liturgy was full of poetry by early Celtic Christians, words that celebrated nature and grace and the light of dawn. As I walked back home, this time cupping a borrowed candle in my hand, I thought of the words of the prophet Isaiah: "The people walking in darkness have seen a great light; on those living in the land of deep darkness a light has dawned" (Isaiah 9:2; cf. Matthew 4:16). And the darkness has never been able to overwhelm it.

That winter I also visited historic sites of spiritual significance in Italy and Turkey (ancient Asia Minor), and participated in some active centers of spiritual practice closer to home. During these travels and afterward, I pored over Scripture and got into the literature of Christian spirituality. The amount and breadth of this latter material proved daunting. The *Classics of Western Spirituality* series, to cite just one example, has already grown to over one hundred volumes, and more are anticipated. Unfinished books soon piled up all around my study, and I began to lose control. The problem was compounded by the fact that many of these writers were advising me not to speed-read, but to slow down and meditate! I realized that the best I could do was survey this vast corpus. Despite the cursory nature of my approach, certain strong and persistent themes began to emerge. In this book I hope to share some of my preliminary observations about them and their implications for the church today.

The Original Design

It will help us appreciate the dynamics of Christian spirituality if first we recall what it means, according to the Christian faith, to be human, and then remember the Scripture's analysis of what is wrong with us now. As we shall see, each dynamic of Christian spirituality addresses an aspect of our pathological human condition, and thereby renews a dimension of God's original design for us.

Among all God's creatures, great and small, we are uniquely like him (Genesis 1:26–27). This makes human life sacred and gives us each great dignity and worth. It's like an old rabbi once put it: Whenever a person walks down the street, we should imagine a cloud of angels out in front shouting, "Make way, make way! Make way for the image of God."[7]

The image of God in us has more than one dimension. To begin, God is triune—experiencing within himself an eternal communion of the persons of the Godhead. So the image of God is first of all a *social* likeness. It indicates an ability to reflect in *our* relations something of the interactive, loving mutuality within the Trinity.

God is also holy and perfect. He is wondrous in his moral character, glorious in his essence and powers. We have the capacity to reflect this holiness and glory, for he has equipped us with qualities and powers that mirror his own, including those of conscience, virtue, intellectual reflection, creativity, and free will. And so we realize that the image of God in us is *substantive* as well. God has crowned us "with glory and honor," and intends for us to be holy and whole as he is.

And finally, God is a God who *acts*—who does things (like creating, sustaining, and redeeming). God's image in us therefore has a *functional* side as well. It involves a capacity for creative work, sovereignty over the rest of creation, and participation in God's own kingdom-building project in history.

SOMETHING WRONG WITH US

Now the bad news—something very serious happened early on in history to mess up our original design. The image of God in us has been seriously defaced, though not entirely erased. We are no longer what we once were. We are shadows of our true selves. We long to become fully human again. But in the meantime, we suffer because the different aspects of the image of God in us have all been distorted. Our root problem is that our souls have become, in Martin Luther's famous phrase, curved inward. We have become self-absorbed and sealed off from what is outside of us.

Here in summary form is the Christian pathology report on the human condition. We were designed for relationship, but every day we experience the opposite reality of *alienation*—of degrees of separation from God and others and even nature itself. Our varied experiences of distance and disconnect create what philosophers describe as the alienated self. This explains why themes of reconciliation, belonging, and community figure so prominently in the gospel.

As indicated earlier, we were also designed to image God's holiness and wholeness. Instead we now live with the realization that we are *damaged* persons. Sometimes Christians assume that the only significant consequence of sin is guilt. Not true. Sin is also enormously destructive, leaving human beings themselves weakened, bound, wounded, and filled with self-loathing. Salvation, as the imagery of the Bible makes clear, is also about *healing*, the progressive rediscovery of our authentic selves, and restoration to wholeness.

Finally, part of the anguish of human existence is our frequent inability to find deep meaning and a profound sense of purpose for living. The question "Why?" haunts us even more intensely as we age, begin to tire, and see our end approaching. It accounts for our longings for significance and our restless gadflying about. There is a simplistic kind of advice going around that we should content ourselves with *being*, and not worry about *doing*. Such advice is always well meant. Nonetheless, it is misleading. We were designed to be doers too, and to derive fulfillment from our efforts. The call to contribute to something that *matters*, to something bigger than our individual selves, is not a duty imposed, but in fact an incredible gift. It is part of what makes our lives meaningful. But now we are ready to consider the dynamics of Christian spirituality—and to see how they each meet a fundamental human need.

THE RELATIONAL DYNAMIC

The first dynamic of Christian spirituality is a *relational* one. There is a God, and there are other people like us; and as humans we share this world with a myriad of other creatures. The fact is that we are not alone. If we try to live in denial of this, we will only slide downward into dysfunction. As Jewish philosopher and mystic Martin Buber declared, "All real living is meeting."[8] Human existence is *essentially* relational.

The impulses of this dynamic move both vertically and horizontally. From the first chapters of the Bible, where Enoch walked faithfully with God (Genesis 5:24), to Jesus' departing assurance that he would be with us always (Matthew 28:20), the Bible attaches great importance to relationship with God. Christians justified by faith in Jesus Christ have an official relationship with God that is established solidly and safely beyond fluctuations in feeling. But this relationship is also meant to be experiential and living—a matter of keeping company with God. It can even develop, incredibly enough, into something akin to *friendship* with God (John 15:15).

Left alone in our sinful state, we tend toward narcissism. We become, in Paul's indicting phrase, lovers of ourselves (2 Timothy 3:2). But once we open ourselves up to God, things begin to change. The life of God, which is characterized by self-giving love, turns out to be infectious. God draws us out of ourselves and "into the grand objective realm of the *not merely me*."[9] God's love, Paul recalled, "has been poured out into our hearts through the Holy Spirit, who has been given to us" (Romans 5:5).

This new experience creates a *general* disposition of openness, so that our souls now have a capacity to connect with, plus an inclination to embrace rather than to exclude, other human beings. Love for God and love for neighbor are two expressions of the same divine impulse.

THE TRANSFORMATIONAL DYNAMIC

Though we exist in relationships, and are profoundly affected by them, we will never *become* the other, nor will we ever be *absorbed into* the other. Our identity will always survive. That's the first thing. The second is that what we are is not what we *ought* to be, nor what we once were. This leads us necessarily to the transformational dynamic of Christian spirituality.

As we have already noted, simply being in relationship begins our transformation. True friendship with God, James Houston points out, is always *transforming* friendship.[10] It never leaves us unchanged. In 2 Corinthians 3:18, the apostle Paul explains this dynamic by drawing an analogy to Moses on Sinai: "We all, who with unveiled faces contemplate the Lord's glory, are being transformed into his image with ever-increasing glory." It is a case of reflected glory.[11]

A great amount of the evil in the world, perhaps the bulk of it, originates within the human spirit—and this toxic wellspring must be repaired. The biblical diagnosis of the human condition is that people need radical renewal from the inside out. This explains why classic Christian spirituality took the challenge of the self so seriously, practiced self-examination, intentionally cultivated virtue, and embraced spiritual disciplines. The goal is the transformation of the heart—the inner command-center of one's entire being. And change is never easy.

But there is another side to this whole story. Sin (whether it is the kind we commit, or the kind committed against us) is never good for us. Its effects are always harmful, disabling, and disfiguring, leaving us as injured victims of a crime. In the end, the Bible warns, sin will always turn bitter and eventually lead to death.

The gospel includes the good news that God is not only our Savior but our *Healer* (Exodus 15:26). He doesn't want us to live permanently with the wounds that sin inflicts. By his grace we are destined to become *whole* as well as holy. *Healer* is one of the great titles for God in the Old Testament. He is the one who heals his people. Time and time again, the prophets promised the people of God that if they would return to him with their whole hearts, he would *heal* their land (2 Chronicles 7:14).

The Vocational Dynamic

From the inner workings of the heart, Jesus explained, flows every decision a person makes, every word they say, every action they perform (Luke 6:43–45). Who we are becoming on the inside naturally and inevitably finds expression in our outward behavior. The Christian life is about connecting and becoming. It is also, finally, about *doing.* The third dynamic of true Christian spirituality is the vocational. This word is derived from the Latin *vocare,* which means "to call." My intent in using it here is to underscore the fact that we have a calling upon our lives to participate in the purposes of God. Authentic Christian spirituality follows the pattern of the incarnation — it becomes flesh. Vocation is following the heart of God into the world.

The conversion biography of the apostle Paul is just one of many biblical stories that illustrate and confirm this threefold pattern of Christian spirituality. On the road to Damascus, Saul encountered Christ in a memorable experience that left him temporarily blind. Immediately he started to undergo a major transformation of his whole life and character, including a total reorientation of his worldview. And following on from this he was eventually commissioned into service as an apostle to the Gentiles. He never got over the privilege of it all.

Paul's story, and the stories of others like him, might lead us to conclude that these are sequential steps in Christian spirituality. But they are *more* than this. They are all continuing, *ongoing realities* of the Christian life. I hope it will become even clearer as we continue that these three dynamics—the relational, transformational, and vocational—are always vitally connected, overlapping, and interdependent. It is not possible to choose one and neglect the others.

Bringing these three themes together as we conclude, we can say that authentic Christian spirituality (or the Christian life, which is the same thing) is a Spirit-enabled relationship with the triune God that results in openness to others, healing progress toward Christlikeness, and willing participation in God's purposes in the world.

The longings of the human spirit are most fully satisfied in Jesus Christ, as we encounter him through his Spirit in the world today. From a Christ-centered perspective, we can say that the first dynamic is about Christ *with* us. The second concerns Christ *in* us, and the third is about Christ working *through* us. By his Spirit, then, Christ is inviting people to come to him, submit to his transforming influence, and then follow him into the world. The pattern is always the same. True spirituality involves continuous cycles of encounter, change, and action.

BACK TO THE IRISH SAINTS

Thomas Cahill warned that if civilization is to be saved, it will not be by modern clones of the administratively astute and technologically advantaged Romans. It will be by *saints*. I thought about this on another stormy evening on Iona, as I walked alone to a stony bay on the west side of the island. There, some suppose, the intrepid Columba and a few other wild Irish friends first blew ashore in their fragile coracles many centuries ago. I gazed on the scene for some time—until I was soaked through and chilled to the bone. I pocketed a little white stone to remember those strange saints, and then turned back toward my lodgings some distance away. As I did, I marveled at their courage. What kind of persons were they? What resources were they accessing? What made them tick?

Some words of Patrick, that great Celtic giant, spoke into my mind as I walked on: "I bind unto myself today the power of God to hold and lead ... Christ be with me, Christ within me ... I bind unto myself the name, the strong name of the Trinity." The answer to my question lies buried in this ancient, mystical, militant imagery. Hopefully we have caught a glimpse of the timeless spiritual dynamics operating behind the saint's evocative words. In the chapters that follow, we will explore these themes more fully.

Chapter Summary

The modern way of life has left the human spirit unsatisfied. Though organized religion has been found wanting, real *Spirit*-uality remains God's gracious provision for the soul-hunger of every age. We have introduced a framework for understanding such spirituality—one that highlights its three essential dynamics. The first, the *relational*, deals with being in healthy relationship to God and others. The second, the *transformational*, examines the sanctifying and healing changes God's Spirit works in our souls. And the third, the *vocational*, considers the new life and mission to which we are called. These three are interconnected, and each is essential to life as God intended it to be.

PART I

THE RELATIONAL DYNAMIC: CHRIST *WITH* US

We were created for community,
but our sin has produced alienation.
By his Spirit, Christ is restoring our intimacy
with God and others.

FRIENDSHIP WITH GOD

Abraham ... was called God's friend.

James 2:23

Geneva is a sophisticated French-speaking city at the west end of Switzerland's largest lake. Its prosperity reflects years of international investment and prudent Swiss banking. Today you'll pay a small fortune for a cup of coffee in Geneva, and a lot more for a Cartier bracelet or Rolex watch. One day I was walking about in the old part of the city, up on the hill that its prehistoric townsfolk had strategically chosen to fortify. As I strolled about, my mind drifted back to an earlier moment in this place's rich history.

I imagined (and some of this really *is* my imagination) how quiet it might have been that night in the seventeenth century when someone snuck past the guards at the city gate. By the light of the moon the shrouded figure walked briskly through the town square, past the public well, and up through the cobblestone streets toward the Gothic cathedral silhouetted against the sky. Minutes later he knocked at the door of Theodore Beza, John Calvin's successor as leader of this influential Protestant city. Removing his cloak, the visitor revealed himself to be Francis de Sales, the exiled Roman Catholic bishop of Geneva. A generation earlier, French and Swiss Protestants under Calvin had taken over the city and sent all the Catholics packing. In a

catastrophic reversal of fortunes for them, the Catholic population
was banned from the city.

It was a time when many people readily thrust one another
through with pikes to advance their personal brand of religion.[1] But
by every account de Sales was a saintly figure. He once cautioned
more violent Catholics that ultimately "love alone will shake the walls
of Geneva."[2] The ambitious goal of de Sales' clandestine visit was to
persuade Beza himself to revert to the Roman Catholic faith. He was
not successful, although one has to admire his boldness and daring.
The real legacy of Francis de Sales rests above the push and shove
of religious conflict. It lies in the fervency of his devotional life, as
articulated in such enduring classics as his *Introduction to the Devout
Life*, and a more challenging treatise *On the Love of God*.

Back in his youth, when the doctrine of predestination was all the
buzz, de Sales had been traumatized by uncertainty about whether he
was already elect to salvation or damned to hell. His personal crisis
was not resolved in the normal evangelical way—through a settled
inner assurance of salvation. Instead, he found soul peace by deciding
to love God while he could, and regardless of God's final determina-
tion of his destiny. As de Sales prayed, "If I am condemned not to love
you in eternity, I can at least love you with all my power during this
life."[3] Thus de Sales' love for God took on a tragic-heroic character.
Despite its lack of assurance, it was incredibly passionate and strong.
And there was a remarkable cheerfulness to it as well. He believed that
love for God should be the true wellspring of everything a Christian
does. Like Jane de Chantel, with whom he worked closely through
the years, his goal was always to cultivate "a deep interior intimacy
with God."[4] Even today, so many years later, he challenges us to think
about *our* relationship to God.

WE ARE NOT ALONE

One conviction supports everything else Christians believe. The
foundation of the entire Christian worldview is the reality of God.
Not more than four words into the Bible you run into it. Genesis starts

out: "In the beginning *God.*" Likewise the Apostles' Creed, a famous early testimony to Christian faith, begins: "*I believe in God* the Father Almighty." Some broad-minded skeptics concede that it can be helpful to *imagine* that there is a God, and to live *as though* this is true. True Christianity considers such an allowance altogether insulting. The writer to the Hebrews considered the existence of God the essential premise of living faith. It seems rather obvious, but whoever wants to come to God must first believe that he exists (Hebrews 11:6). The Bible says that God *is.* And this means that we are not alone.

And here is a related truth. The God who is also speaks. He communicates in word and deed. Francis Schaeffer, the Christian apologist and prophetic critic of modern culture who established L'Abri Fellowship in Switzerland, captured this truth in a memorable declaration. "He is there," Schaeffer said of God—that's the first truth. And then he added, "And he is not silent." God has spoken in the past, and *he still speaks.* The voice of God still reaches out to connect with human beings. In this lies the possibility of relationship.

CREATED FOR RELATIONSHIP

The triune God is a relational community. From all eternity the Father, Son, and Holy Spirit have been relating to one another in an atmosphere of loving mutuality. Suppose for a moment, silly as it sounds, that God could be the object of a scientific experiment. Imagine scientists in white coats performing a biopsy on the Trinity. Visualize them returning to their lab with a small sample of the interior ether of God. What would they find? They would discover that their sample contained holy, self-giving love. Because that's what God is like. And then the Bible tells us that God decided to create humans. They arrive, as he intended, bearing a special likeness to himself. And part of what this means is that we too are designed for relationship.

Why did God create people? He certainly had no *need* for us. A classic answer is that God created people to glorify himself—to enhance his own magnificent luster by having more beings around to sing his praises and do his bidding. It is hard to explain this without making God sound rather egocentric. The opportunity to create billions of admirers sounds appealing enough to us. Which one of us would not jump at a chance to do the same?

But we get closer to the truth when we see that his creative act was an expression of his loving heart. Throughout history the heart of God, by its very nature, has always been stretching to incorporate more persons into its ever-widening embrace of commitment and caring. Amazingly, such love is not diluted or diminished by expansion. We find its analogy in the love that brings a couple together in marriage. In time they may choose to widen the locus of their love to include children. Their love for one another is not weakened in the least by making room for these others.

It makes sense that God lovingly wills other creatures into existence so they also can enjoy what he has already been experiencing within himself. The joy of God's own loving mutuality is simply too good not to share. Without ever becoming God ourselves, we are invited to enter into relationship with him and thus "participate in the divine nature" (2 Peter 1:4). This is all for God's glory and our good.

But relationship with God has become difficult for us. The first problem, as we have already noted, is the inward curve of our sinful selves. Unfortunately our narcissist bent is reinforced by the individualistic spirit of Western culture. We Westerners do not do relationships very well because they are seldom our highest priorities. We are more concerned with mastering our environment or improving ourselves. Self-improvement is a worthy goal, but problems arise when we treat relationships as mere means to this end. Too often we size up people according to their usefulness to us. And we tend to treat God the same.

Hectic *busyness* is another obstacle to relationship with God. The emerging global economy is more competitive than anything the world has yet seen. As a result, we feel the pressure to be relentlessly busy and productive. This imposed pace of life keeps us exhausted and thoroughly preoccupied with things that are trivial and passing.

Busyness shrinks the chronological and psychological space we have left over for God in our lives.

KNOWING GOD'S TRUE CHARACTER

The English poet Samuel Taylor Coleridge once observed: "He prayeth well, who loveth well." What did he mean? I think Coleridge meant that how we pray, and how often we pray, are affected by our mental and emotional image of the God with whom we are dealing. If we deeply admire, love, and trust God, we will find ourselves drawn very naturally and willingly into prayer and praise. If, on the other hand, we do not perceive him to be attractive or inviting, we will perform our duty halfheartedly at best. We will pray neither well nor very frequently.

Nothing affects our relationship with God more than our perception of him. A. W. Tozer reminds us that this is perhaps the most important indicator of how we will live our lives.[5] James Houston concurs: "Tell me who is your God, and I will tell you how you pray."[6] If we nurse an image of God as stern, incessantly demanding, and punitive, we will feel afraid and wary of him. We may carry wounds from the past that we more or less blame on him, and so we feel resentment and a silent coolness.

Such feelings are rooted in a serious misperception of God. The most important realization we can come to in life is that "God is good for us."[7] Whatever our longings may be for truth, goodness, or beauty, they will be satisfied by moving toward the eternal source of these things rather than away from him. God wills our good and blessing, and he calls for our obedience because he wants to see these things become realities for us. As one writer has so beautifully put it, "Our happiness is important to God."[8]

Self-giving love is at the core of God's nature. The inspired biblical imagery for communicating this reality is that God is a loving parent—specifically, a heavenly *Father*. Jesus himself taught us, in the Lord's Prayer, to address God this way. Yet this analogy between God's character and human fatherhood can be problematic for those who have had strained relationships with their human fathers. Because of the flaws of those who cared for them, even the term "father" can make them bristle.

Should we assume that the imagery of fatherhood is useless in their case? Not at all. It is freeing to realize that God is the *ideal* father who may have eluded us in our childhood development and earthly family relationships. He is the one who meets all those longings left unfulfilled by our human parents. When we see him as he really is, then we can truly love God with all our heart and soul and strength (Deuteronomy 6:5).

WE BELONG TO GOD

On one level, the Christian's relationship with God is positional and official. It involves things like the privilege of being justified—of being declared righteous—by God, and adopted into his family. It is about having a new status on the basis of Christ's atoning work that guarantees us an inheritance still to come. The apostle Peter reminded his Gentile readers that prior to their conversion to Christ they were not a people at all, but now they were the people of God (1 Peter 2:10). The apostle's language echoes the incredible invitation of God in the Old Testament: "They will be my people, and I will be their God" (Jeremiah 24:7; cf. Zechariah 8:8).

This is the language of covenant—one of the most important themes in the entire Scriptures. Covenants involve reciprocal commitments, and they create conditions of *belonging* that meet our deepest needs for connection and security. The European Christians who drafted the Heidelberg Catechism in the sixteenth century asked their children to identify their only comfort (or, greatest consolation) in life and in death. Then they taught them to answer: "That I *belong*— body and soul, in life and in death—not to myself but to my faithful savior Jesus Christ."[9]

To be the people of God means that God has made a commitment to us. And so, "though my father and mother forsake me, the LORD will receive me" (Psalm 27:10). One of the special ministries of the Holy Spirit is to assure us that this is really so — that it is not just a product of our wishful thinking. "The Spirit himself testifies with our spirit that we *are* God's children" (Romans 8:16) — that we belong to God.

FRIENDSHIP WITH GOD

The relational dynamic also involves the blessing of God's presence. Years ago, when we were studying in Scotland, we became friends with another student couple from Finland. They had a little baby, and like us, were financially challenged. One winter evening these Finnish friends began talking about how much they missed being home for Christmas. Their extended family always gathered together to celebrate the season. Outside the wind might be howling and the snow blowing, but indoors the entire family — from great-grandparents to newborn babies — would sit around the perimeter of a warm living room. "Sometimes a whole hour would go by without anyone saying a word," our friend assured us with nostalgia. "We just soaked up all the unspoken love, grateful to be together."

We were incredulous. Could even Nordic people be *that* quiet in group settings? Nevertheless, the image of those Finnish family gatherings stuck with us. It reminds us that a relationship doesn't require incessant conversation. There is a dimension of communion that exists even in the absence of speaking. Relationship with God can involve treasured moments of ecstasy, revelation, and signs of the supernatural. But equally important are those longer stretches of the peace that passes all understanding, and the awareness that it is well with our soul. Then we begin to experience for ourselves the comfortable connection the poet Emily Dickinson had in view when, without any disrespect, she referred to the hospitable face of "our old neighbor God."[10]

But there is even more than this. The relational dynamic is also about *keeping company with God*, staying alert and responsive to his voice. It is about being in harmony, enjoying oneness of purpose and intent. It is the experience described in Brother Lawrence's late medieval classic, *The Practice of the Presence of God*.

Encountering God tends to evoke reverence and awe. Isaiah spoke for all worshipers when he cried out: "Woe to me! ... I am ruined! For I am a man of unclean lips ... and my eyes have seen the King, the LORD Almighty" (Isaiah 6:5). It is all the more astonishing, then, to read in Scripture that Abraham was called God's friend, and that the privilege of friendship with God is extended to us as well. "I have called you friends," says Jesus, "for everything that I learned from my Father I have made known to you" (John 15:15).

Does this mean that we should no longer contemplate God with awe? Has God the Father Almighty properly morphed into the Omni-Dude? We have to unpack the imagery of "friendship" very carefully. Its essence is not informality or—heaven forbid—jocularity. The language of divine friendship gives us permission to add to our sustained reverence for God an enjoyment of full acceptance, deep intimacy, and safe disclosure.

We all know how demeaning it is when a controlling boss, teacher, or parent micromanages everything we do, constantly looking over our shoulder. Such an interpersonal style alienates us from those persons who have more power than us. The way they use their authority is destructive to our mutual relationship. This is certainly true of marriages as well. If a husband (or wife) usurps an asymmetrical amount of the power and decision making, it erodes the level of happiness in the relationship. The dynamics of control are always inversely related to the quality of a friendship. For the sake of his relationship to us, God deliberately restrains his rightful power to control all outcomes and decisions. He gives us the freedom to choose, either for or against his will, without coercion. It's one of the risks God takes so that instead of being his powerless servants we can truly become his friends.

SPEAKING AND *Listening*

Shortly after we were married, my wife and I splurged on dinner out at an upscale hotel. As we ate, soaked up the luxurious atmosphere, and talked together, we noticed an obviously well-to-do older couple at a table nearby. Each fixated on the food in front of them, pursing their lips to cool the soup on their spoons, chewing their meat, wiping their mouths with linen napkins. Not a word passed between them. When they weren't eating, they just stared off into space, avoiding all eye contact. It was not the atmosphere of wordless communion, not exactly the warm Finnish family Christmas I earlier described. The lack of table talk chilled us as newlyweds. What a troubling prospect that a marriage could deteriorate until a husband and wife no longer had anything to say to each another. Communication is natural and essential to a living relationship.

Some years later we were in a restaurant and noticed another couple—much younger, this time—and the dynamic of their relationship was strikingly different. One of them was speaking with great animation, nonstop, scarcely ever taking a breath. The other sat completely mute and, it seemed to us, totally bored. The person never made a response. There was no opportunity, really. Once I think I saw the silent partner roll their eyes. That was it. We concluded that this relationship was in trouble too, because healthy relationships are interactive, never exclusively one-way. They involve dialogue—give and take. The same is true with God. When we tend to do all the talking, mostly in the form of hurried petitions, it serves to illustrate that we have likely not cultivated the complementary art of *listening* to what he may be trying to say to us.

Spirit-attuned Christians are attentive to what is happening all around them, and the voice of God in the midst of it all. Spiritual persons are not always charging forward with their ears pinned back. Their minds are not so totally closed that they no longer need to hear anything. They are quiet but alert. Both Isaiah and Jesus mourned the phenomena of persons with ears, but an inability to hear (Isaiah 6:9–10; Matthew 13:13). They were referring to the tragedy of having a God-given potential for discerning attentiveness, but refusing to develop and use it.

ON THE RIVER HILLS

We were living in western Canada, and I was about to make the biggest vocational decision of my life. To accept the opportunity that had come up would require that I resign my job and oblige our whole family to uproot and move to another city. The stakes were high. About this time I happened to be traveling not so very far from Outlook, the small town where I had lived in my teenage years. It was a special place overlooking the South Saskatchewan River valley that winds its way for hundreds of miles in a northeasterly direction across the flat prairies from the Rocky Mountains to the salt water of Hudson's Bay. The valley is probably a couple of miles across, and consists of hills descending from both sides down to the river in the middle. As a teenager, I used to carry a .22 rifle and walk those hills—pondering the issues of adolescent life and praying to God. The wind was always blowing. The smell of sage, the ubiquitous gopher holes, and the prickly little cactus plants wedged down in the short spear grass still materialize in my mind as I think back to that time and place.

It had been at least twenty-five years, and a lot of water under the bridge, but I felt the need to return to that "sacred space." I parked beside the highway, climbed a fence, and began to walk down toward the river hills. The Saskatchewan wind was blowing, as always, and the leaves of the poplar trees flashed and clattered in response. I had my list of petitions ready—for guidance, discernment, safety, finances, children's welfare, proper timing, and more. It was a long and predictable litany of midlife cares and concerns.

Eventually I found my way to the crest of one particular knoll, and sensed that this was the old place. As I opened my heart to start my monologue, a strange thing happened. I couldn't speak. The details of my concerns faded away, or rather were swept away, by an inrushing, liquid flood of feeling that I was able eventually to recognize as gratitude. Through these many years of coming and going, I realized that I had been watched over and protected by an unseen presence.

An overflowing sense of thankfulness welled up in me, strong and unexpected. It was like a hand clamped over my mouth, preventing me from voicing my requests. I stood there for some time, basking in a profound and wordless assurance that God was good and all would be well. The water moving silently below me was like the river glorious we sing about in church, a symbol of God's perfect peace. Eventually

I climbed back up the hill, aware that my plan to hold a summit with God, and speak my mind, had been completely thwarted. Instead of speaking, I had been spoken to. The experience branded in my memory that the Christian life is indeed a relationship in which *both* parties get their turns to speak.

THE SUFFICIENCY OF THIS RELATIONSHIP

Healthy marriage and family dynamics are a blessing at every stage of life, and so are the social dynamics of a healthy workplace and church, and valued friendships with other human beings. But there are times in our journeys through life when the support of other humans falls away, and we have only God on our side. Death, misunderstandings, and a host of other variables can drive wedges between us and our companions in life — even those closest to us.

During those times, we discover the sufficiency of our relationship with God, that even by itself it is enough to sustain us. In this spirit the psalmist wrote: "My flesh and my heart may fail, but God is the strength of my heart and *my portion forever*" (Psalm 73:26). God is the psalmist's discerning choice, because this choice provides for all his deepest needs.

Christians who have experienced this truth about our relationship with God gain personal strength. They are no longer terrified by the prospect of being alone. Social pressure loses some of its power over them. When they enter into community, their action is rooted in choice rather than desperate need. In the imagery of Henri Nouwen, the ragged pain of loneliness is succeeded by the serenity of solitude.[11]

GOD MUST BE FIRST

Centuries ago people assumed that the sun revolved around the earth. In view of its daily westward arc from sunrise to sunset, this seemed eminently reasonable. In the sixteenth century, astronomers Galileo and Copernicus stimulated an enormous controversy by arguing, with mathematical support, that in fact the earth revolved around the sun. The claims of these scientists shook the world. Their discovery called for a paradigm shift in thinking—a complete reorientation to reality. It demanded that people replace their earth-centered perception of the solar system with a sun-centered one. Minor changes are manageable for people in good mental health. But paradigm shifts are never easy, even for the healthiest and most flexible among us.

Supremacy belongs to God. Those who discover that he is real can never live again like people who are not yet aware of him. God—by reason of being God—is destined for preeminence in the universe. In the spiritual solar system, we revolve around God, rather than God revolving around us. The Renaissance astronomers' discovery was not accepted without a fight. And realizing that we are not the center of the universe—that God is—can be even more difficult to acknowledge, because so much ego is at stake.

It is counterintuitive that we can find more joy in a God-centered universe than in a self-centered one. But this is, paradoxically, how things really work. God must be first. That is how the universe is designed to run, and when we fight it, everything about our lives gets syncopated, stuttering, and unnatural. When we accept our rightful place in the grand scheme of things, as subordinate rather than supreme, we discover our destiny and our true happiness. Respect for God is the cornerstone of worship, and the beginning of wisdom. Jesus set us the ultimate example of how to live when he said to the Father, "Not my will, but yours be done."

RECIPROCATING DELIGHT

One day I slipped into the back of a British classroom where an old theologian in a black gown was lecturing to a roomful of university undergrads. He announced he was going to try that day to unpack what love was all about—particularly the love of God. The situation didn't look promising as he started to expound the characteristics of divine love in a kind of ascending order. But he grew more impassioned and eloquent as he developed his theme. And by then the students—some of whom were still hung over from the previous night—were drinking it in.

The lecture reached its climax when the professor declared that love always *delights* in the object of its affection. I thought back to various Old Testament assurances that God really does delight in his people (for example, Psalm 149:4). He rejoices over them with singing, says the prophet Zephaniah (3:17). And I thought of that moment at the Jordan River, when Jesus came up out of the muddy-brown waters, and a voice from heaven announced: "This is my Son, whom I love; with him I am well pleased" (Matthew 3:17).

Well pleased! What an incredible validation moment for Jesus—to know that he was the object of the Father's approval and pleasure. We wish that we had been in his sandals. Yet in a sense we are. Because of what Christ has done for us, and our identification with him, the Father gazes with similar delight on us. Even longtime Christians can get a bit emotional when this truth really sinks in. Somewhere along the weary line we gave up hope of such a thing being possible. But it's true, and incredibly freeing when we get hold of it. It evokes the same feeling toward God in us. Indeed our relationship with God reaches its highest point and fulfillment in an atmosphere of *reciprocating* delight.

Francis de Sales knew quite a bit about delighting in God. But the greatest thing in the world is to combine what he knew and experienced with the blessed assurance (which to some extent eluded him all his saintly life) that through Christ we *belong* to God, and will for all eternity. That is a joy the heart simply cannot contain, and which, as we will see in the next chapter, spills over into our other relationships as well.

SOME HELPFUL GUIDES

BERNARD OF CLAIRVAUX (1090 – 1153 AD)

Bernard was one of the greatest spiritual leaders of the Middle Ages. His experience of joy through intimacy with God has been memorialized in his little classic, *On Loving God* (ca 1130 AD). It is even more fully explored in his commentary on the biblical Song of Songs. Yet his quest for intimacy with God did not isolate him from secular life. He was a vigorous administrator and an active (and controversial) commentator on the political issues of his day.

A. W. TOZER (1897 – 1963)

Tozer was a simple, self-educated Midwesterner who began his working life in an Akron, Ohio rubber factory. Remarkably, he came in contact with the literature of Christian mysticism, absorbed it deeply, and then, with a uniquely engaging style (half Jeremiah, half Mark Twain), passed along his discovered insights to countless soul-hungry Americans. Two of his many works, *The Pursuit of God* and *The Knowledge of the Holy*, remain classics still in print.

JOHN PIPER

John Piper is a Minnesota pastor with a strongly Reformed vision of God's glory. In many works, but perhaps especially in his acclaimed work *Desiring God*, Piper develops the theme of the soul's satisfaction in God alone, and the experience of delighting in God as the ultimate source of truth, goodness, and beauty. The heading on his website is that "God is most glorified in us when we are most satisfied with him."

CHAPTER SUMMARY

The first of Christian spirituality's three essential dynamics is the relational. It begins with the realization that we are not alone—that there is a God, and he is not silent. Through Christ and his Spirit, God gives us a new standing before him, and draws us into experiences of his unspoken presence and even into interactive encounters with him. The confidence that God is good for us draws us to, and keeps us in, this vertical communion. What opens up before us is the possibility of a friendship with God characterized by reciprocating delight. In the next chapter, on the topic of experiencing community, we will treat our *horizontal* relationships with others and with creation.

EXPERIENCING COMMUNITY

Dear friends, let us love one another, for love comes from God.
Everyone who loves has been born of God and knows God.

1 John 4:7

The monks at St. Andrew's Benedictine Abbey, in the high desert north of Los Angeles, were delighted to learn of my pending pilgrimage to Italy. "But you *must* visit Subiaco," they insisted. One brother headed for his room and brought back a coffee-table volume full of pictures of it. "This is where our founder, St. Benedict, lived for three years as a hermit back in the sixth century," he explained eagerly. "You have to promise that you'll see it. It's incredible." So a couple of months later, on a sunny morning, I was on a bus heading east out of Rome, climbing toward a ridge of mountains that runs north-south the length of the country, en route to Subiaco to fulfill my promise to the monks back in California. The bus carried us, with lurching gear changes, through some stunningly beautiful towns perched on cliffs. We wound around canyons and through forests until our destination came into view.

From the bus station I still had a hike ahead of me. Just beyond the built-up area of town the road began to climb steeply in switchback fashion. At the base were the ruins of notorious Roman emperor Nero's lavish summer palace, now a neglected patch of stones and blocks overgrown with grass and weeds. I took some comfort from the

thought that Benedict's legacy has fared much better than Nero's—
two large, active monasteries on the mountain I was now ascending,
and a global influence beyond calculation.

Almost fifteen hundred years ago Benedict chose to isolate himself from human contact to pursue life with God. He decided, in other
words, to become a hermit. Benedict selected a tiny cave, really just an
indentation in the side of a massive rock face rising hundreds of feet
from a river valley below. Shepherds up above, so the stories go, would
periodically drop down food to him in a basket tied to a rope. And so
he existed there for three full years—all alone with God.

I finally made it to the top—perspiring and seriously out of breath.
But the view was panoramic. Benedict had a good eye for location.
Today a monastery, impressively engineered to hang on the cliff face,
completely covers over the little cave itself. Unfortunately the building was already closed for the afternoon, and my return bus schedule
did not permit me the luxury of waiting around until it reopened. So
I chose the lesser of two evils and proceeded to bother the monks. I
pressed the buzzer. My trump card was that I had read Benedict's rule
and knew that it requires Benedictines to show hospitality to strangers. I was not disappointed. With only a slight reproachful reminder
that it was not yet time for visitors, the portly monk who opened the
wooden door offered to show me around. Inside we descended right
to Benedict's little ledge itself. I reached out to the dark stones in the
flicker of candlelight and touched the distant past.

But as history also records, Benedict did not stay there. After
three years, he concluded that life with God was best pursued in community rather than in isolation, that the monastery was superior to the
hermit's cave. The experience of being loved by God, and loving him
back, grows naturally into love for others. The relational dynamic of
Christian spirituality moves horizontally as well as vertically. Benedict climbed down from Subiaco and went south to Monte Cassino,
another mountaintop site. There he wrote his famous "rule" for those
who wished to join his community, and established what has become
the motherhouse of the international Benedictine order. He testi-

fied that authentic Christian spirituality is also about experiencing community.

In this chapter we move on, like Benedict, to our horizontal relationships. What I hope to demonstrate is that this is not a new topic, but an extension of our previous one. Love for God and love for others amount, really, to one thing. What unites them is the virtue of openness to the "not merely *me*." Our personal fulfillment and destiny are found by taking our place, and playing our part, in a larger web of relationships. We may hesitate to move into this larger sphere from fear that we may be diminished. But such fear is misplaced. Moving in this direction is essential to our fulfillment and joy.

NO ONE IS AN ISLAND

We have already noted that the triune God is a relational community. Throughout eternity the Father, Son, and Holy Spirit have existed in a loving, interactive unity. Eventually God created humans in his own likeness, and an important aspect of this is that we are designed, like God, for relationship. In the last chapter, we considered how this makes it possible for us to connect with God. Now we turn our attention to the way our Godlike capacity for relationship plays itself out in human interactions and in our interface with the rest of the created order. It is God's plan that we should experience community with others and harmony with nature.

We tend to categorize some people as more relational than others. We call such folks "people persons." To cite a rather overworked classification system, we think of people as extroverts or introverts. It is true that people have different comfort levels when it comes to things like hospitality or solitude. But the important thing to remember is that these are merely distinctions of temperament.

God does not favor one temperament over another, even though Western culture and many churches seem to. It is not his intent to change quiet, thoughtful people into gregarious dynamos. As God's image-bearers, we are all designed for connection with others. Extroverts may know more people, but introverts often forge deeper and more enduring relationships. In the famous words of poet John Donne, "No man [or woman] is an island."[1] We are meant to live our lives with a disposition of openness to others. To live this way is a key to becoming fully human.

CORRECTING THE CENTRIFUGAL FORCE OF SIN

Unfortunately there are obstacles to the fulfillment of our social destiny. In the last chapter, we noted some serious challenges to growing a high-quality relationship with God: the chronic curvature of our sinful selves, the reinforcing ideology of Western individualism, and the hectic busyness of modern society. All these factors work against experiencing human community as well. And there is another obstructing factor to consider here—the centrifugal tendency of sin.

I first learned about centrifugal force as a child on a playground roundabout, a poorer version of a merry-go-round that consisted of a little circular platform surrounded with a railing. By pushing hard while we ran around in a deeply worn circle we'd get it going as fast as possible. Then we'd try to climb on. Once we did, it wouldn't take long for some of us to begin feeling nauseous. That increased our risk of injury. If we let go, you see, we would instantly find ourselves catapulted out beyond the spinning piece of equipment and into the nearby bushes. Centrifugal force propels objects outward from the center.

Sin is like this. It separates people from one another, pushing them out from a united center in a myriad of isolating directions. Sexism, racism, divisions in families, breakups in marriages, and unjust economic systems that divide people into different classes are just a few of sin's familiar effects. Sin can turn potentially close friends into distant strangers. It creates distance instead of generating mergers. It divides and alienates.

Many expressions of our sinful nature, which the apostle Paul lists in his epistle to the Galatians, are relationally divisive, among them "hatred, discord, jealousy, fits of rage, selfish ambition, dissensions, factions and envy" (5:20–21). The lethal potential of the unrestrained "self" is clearly portrayed in these ominous words. By contrast, grace is a centripetal force. It works in the opposite direction. It takes people divided by misunderstandings, differences, and wounds, and draws them back together in a restored center. The good news is that *shalom*—the desire of the Jewish people throughout their long and troubled history—can become reality again.

THE MALAYSIAN TURTLE

I was viewing the beachfront of the seminary property in Penang, Malaysia, looking at the rocks and coastline that had been spared the brunt of the recent tsunami. Timothy, the preschool child of a student couple, ran up to show me his pet tortoise, Toby. It was obvious he felt great pride and deep affection for it. I took the weight of it in my hands. It was pretty enough, with symmetrical markings of black, green, and yellow. Yet there was absolutely no movement, no indication even of a pulse. I assumed the turtle was alive, but it was hard to tell by looking at it. It was a solid orb of protective plating—no feet exposed, no tail, not even a hint of a head. Everything was sealed up tight. I might as well have been holding a bowling ball.

"Where is he?" I asked, turning the turtle all around and upside down.

Timothy pointed to the underside of the beautiful dark green shell. "He's in there," he said.

"Why doesn't he come out, then?" I asked.

"Toby is afraid," my little friend explained soberly. "He doesn't feel it's safe to come outside right now." So we left Toby on the ground and went off to do other things.

Sometimes we are like that turtle. We are afraid of being hurt, so we close in on ourselves. This is especially true if we have been deeply injured in the past. Then it becomes doubly difficult to become vulnerable to others. The natural tendency of the wounded self is to set up protective barriers to further harm. Tragically, these barriers also prevent the restoration of our true humanity.

We must find the courage to become open again to others. It is not easy. It requires an intervention of the Holy Spirit. We are needy people, and we find our own needs a full-time preoccupation. It is difficult to change the default settings of our psyches, to break free of entrenched habits.

Later we came back to where we had left Toby the turtle on the grass. Now he had disappeared. Evidently he had concluded that the coast was clear, and it was okay for him to come out of his shell. He'd gone quite a distance, up the hill and into the bushes, before we finally tracked him down again. His impressive mobility reminded me that all sorts of adventures are possible if we are willing to move out of our shells.

Two Vectors from a Single Matrix

Jesus was once asked to identify the greatest command of all (Matthew 22:34–40). For his answer he quoted two separate Old Testament texts. First, drawing from Deuteronomy 6 he replied: "Love the Lord your God with all your heart." Then he added, quoting Leviticus 19: "Love your neighbor as yourself." These are not two completely distinct commands, randomly thrown together to sum up the Christian's moral obligation. They are actually two vectors from a single matrix — a restored capacity to look beyond oneself.[2]

The passion of Walter Rauschenbusch, an American pastor from an immigrant German family, was for a Christianity that met the needs of the soul while addressing the problems of the world. He found it tough sledding to get his comfortable New York City church members to feel concern for those suffering in nearby slums. He chafed against the selfish individualism that appeared to persist even — and sometimes especially — among confessing Christians.

These were people, he reflected, who had responded positively to the evangelical gospel offer of forgiveness of sins and the free gift of eternal life. It gradually dawned on him that their "conversions" had required from them no significant change in their basic orientation to life. In an indictment of this kind of Christian faith commitment, he wrote: "To be afraid of hell or purgatory and desirous of a life without pain or trouble in heaven [is] not in itself Christian. It [is] self-interest on a higher level."[3]

Rauschenbusch believed that the essence of sin was selfishness, and the only sure sign of authentic conversion and regeneration was a turning to God *and* humanity. As he saw things, "the sense of solidarity [with others] is one of the distinctive marks of the true followers of Jesus." The essence of conversion was, for him, to align one's life "in obedience to the loving impulses of the spirit of God."[4]

Bona fide unselfishness is indeed evidence of the supernatural at work. I have a cartoon from the *New Yorker* magazine of a middle-aged couple leaving church together. "How can I love my enemies," the husband complains, "when I don't even like my friends?" Such candor is amusing, but also challenging, because it comes so close to the truth. The apostle John reminds us that "love comes from God" (1 John 4:7). That's how it is possible to love one another—it grows out of our relationship with him. A soul is forever changed by opening itself up to the life of God. It is possible, the apostle Peter explains, for us to "participate in the divine nature" (2 Peter 1:4). Through persistent formation, loving openness to others can become a fixed disposition of our hearts.

The Spirit and the Welcoming Self

Another way of understanding the welcoming self is to consider the uniting work of the Holy Spirit. On one occasion the apostle Paul urged the believers in Ephesus: "Make every effort to keep the unity of the Spirit through the bond of peace" (Ephesians 4:3). The Spirit's mission is to create such unity among believers. His mission is to facilitate peace—the same *shalom* that has been so elusive in human relationships through the millennia. The Spirit is a divine counterbalance to the signature effects of sin. The Holy Spirit creates space in me for the other.

Miroslav Volf, a Croatian well acquainted with the realities of human hatred and violence in his former homeland, has eloquently presented the options we have when faced with otherness: exclusion or embrace. The first is "an unflinching will to exclude," symbolized by arms tightly crossed and closed. The alternative—embrace—involves two body movements. Open arms, reminiscent of Christ's outstretched arms on the cross and the Father's welcome home of the prodigal son, illustrate the desire for inclusion—the "sign of discontent at being myself only." But there is also a closing of the arms around the other, symbolizing both incorporation and enrichment. The one embraced, he maintains, not only enters within the circle of care but "become[s] part of me so that she can enrich me with what she has and I do not."[5] This completes what Henri Nouwen has described as the Spirit-led progression from hostility to hospitality.

FORGIVENESS: THE GRACE TO START OVER

We are sinners, and the consequences of our sinning spread like blood in water. Inevitably we experience its painful effects in our relationships. When we hurt someone else, we try to rationalize our actions. When others hurt us, we seek revenge, and a vicious, unending cycle of violence develops. We watch movies where Mafia families destroy each other this way. We know that there are tribes that have annihilated themselves in this way. But it goes beyond the Mafia and tribal cultures—it is the story of us all.

This is where forgiveness, the response Jesus modeled, must enter the picture. It releases the culprit in such a way that the cycle can stop. It is the blessed grace of a new relational start. It provides an opportunity to put a negative series of events into reverse, to back up and start over again in the right direction. We have been taught to pray: "Forgive us our debts, as we also have forgiven our debtors" (Matthew 6:12). Forgive, Jesus urges, just as I have forgiven you.

We have to keep in mind that forgiveness is not something easily or instantly achieved. It is a slow and painful resolve that must be sustained with great discipline over long periods of time.[6] Christ made our willingness to forgive others a prerequisite to experiencing his forgiving grace in our own lives. Surely he considers acceptable anyone's sincere intent and desire to fully forgive, even though a long journey still lies between them and complete victory.

Yet despite the centrality of forgiveness in Christianity, confusion persists about what it means to forgive another person. Two definitions presently compete. The first, the *therapeutic* one, recognizes the healing benefits to a victim of "forgiving" the perpetrator in the sense of finally "letting it go." It involves relinquishing all claims to further compensation. The essential thing is that the victim be freed to move on.

The other understanding is *restorative* forgiveness, and this I think comes closest to the Christian ideal. It aims beyond the healing of a victim to the rebuilding of relational harmony between the estranged parties. Certain conditions must be met, of course, before this goal can be fully realized, and no one party can unilaterally create all the necessary conditions. As a result, full restoration is not always possible. Nonetheless it remains the ideal toward which the act of forgiveness aims. Its hope is that the conditions for full trust could somehow be restored.

The Church as Prototype

No one can come to God and remain detached from other Christians. The New Testament is very clear on this. "We were all baptized by one Spirit so as to form one body" (1 Corinthians 12:13). Spirit baptism initiates us into both the saving merits of Christ *and* the community of faith. There is only "one baptism," and this is how it works. It is an initiation into both vertical and horizontal relational realities.

Have you ever been to a major car show? The automobile manufacturers show up to tantalize the public with shiny, fully loaded versions of their most appealing vehicles. Consumers get to ask questions, kick tires, and sit behind the wheel. The real showstoppers are always the concept cars not yet available in car dealerships; stunning creations that reflect the very latest in research and development. Usually only a very few exist yet. It will be years before they will be in full production. But they represent the future.

The church is to be a *prototype* of the coming kingdom of God. It is intended to be a countercultural community in which members build *shalom* by showing respect, and practicing patience, forgiveness, kindness, affirmation, understanding, and inclusion. Neither tactics of control, nor status distinctions that contribute to traditional human hierarchies, is to make a difference here. The unity God promises cannot be achieved by shrewd human leaders. It is a logic-defying gift of the Spirit. The relational dynamics within the church are to serve as a hopeful preview of how all things will someday be when Jesus reigns. The church is to be ahead of the curve.

It is easy, especially for clergy, to get caught up in a dream of the church as a powerful institution, large in numbers and mighty in societal clout. Such a vision is best advanced, of course, by hiring religious CEOs rather than true pastors. But whenever we embrace that vision, it becomes easier to treat the members as disposable means to an end. The biblical vision of the church is far less institutional — much more along the lines of a spiritual community. As David Benner so winsomely reminds us, "Spiritual communities are, after all, simply networks of spiritual friends."[7]

Some Christians today view the church primarily as a herald of the gospel.[8] A herald's job, of course, is to publicly proclaim a message far and wide for all to hear. According to this model, the church's chief responsibility and reason for existence is get the gospel message *out*. If necessary — and here's the key point — the quality of its inner life can be sacrificed for the sake of the greater good, which is the disseminating of its propositional message (that is, its message of words) of good news.

However, it is much more biblical to view the church, as we have been discussing — as a prototype of how God intends for people to relate to one another. God intends for it to embody his real and reconciling presence. One of the key ways it testifies to the reality of God is to do relationships in a different, better way. The herald model focuses on diffusing information. The prototype model is committed to making the truth credible, persuasive, and compelling. How we live in relationship is often more important than what we say. How we live together in community ought to be *in itself* good and hopeful news.

OUR RELATIONSHIP TO THE REST OF CREATION

A few weeks ago I was settled comfortably in my pew, my eyes devoutly closed during the pastoral prayer. I heard the minister ask God that we might somehow learn to leave lighter footprints on his good earth. It was a nice turn of phrase, but it startled me. Immediately my thoughts hurtled back thirty years to my summer job in northern Canada. I had been hired as a deckhand on a large tugboat pushing pods of barges down the mighty Mackenzie River toward the Arctic Ocean. The barges were loaded with oil exploration equipment—trucks, generators, derricks, "mud" boxes, and miles of drill pipe for boring deep into the earth.

Periodically we would run the barges up against the shore and drive the machinery off to designated sites on the fragile tundra. There the caches of equipment would sit until the winter, when crews would fly in and begin operations. I remembered one day awkwardly driving a huge diesel rig off the barge. It groaned under the weight of heavy-duty equipment on its trailer as we crawled along the pristine flats covered in tiny wildflowers and compact grass. The ground was soft above the permafrost, and the tires left a trail maybe six inches deep. On the way back to the ship, one of the old sailors leaned over and told me that the snaking scars my truck had left would probably remain there at least as long as I lived. Winter returned with flurries that August, and I tried to console my conscience that the ruts I'd made would be the first to fill up white as snow.

Human sin destroys not only human relations. It has also driven a wedge between us and nature. The effects of our abuse of the environment are becoming ominous; we are putting at risk nature's ability to sustain our race. As C. S. Lewis has said, our supposed conquest of nature is, in the end, nature's conquest of humanity.[9] What is the solution? More than one person has observed that the global environmental crisis is ultimately a spiritual matter.

A while ago I was asked to lecture on Christianity and the environment at a university in the People's Republic of China. The Chinese are well aware that environmental destruction is a great threat to their nation's future. Which ideological or religious option today—Communism, Confucianism, Taoism, Buddhism, or Christianity—the students wanted to know, offers them the most hope for the future? Which one, they asked, has the best resources for establishing a sustainable long-term relationship to nature?

The prevailing prejudice in the secular West is that Christianity values human life at the expense of everything else. Some Westerners who care deeply about the planet are now seeking support from the enchanted worldview of neo-paganism, the virtue of harmony pursued by Taoists, and the simple, gentle demeanor cultivated in Buddhism.

I suggested to the Chinese students that authentic Christianity is still the best hope for humanity and the natural order that sustains us. But I also admitted that not enough Christians have lived up to the best insights of their faith on environmental issues. The real message of the Bible is not domination and exploitation, but careful stewardship of earth's resources (Genesis 1:26). God judged his creation to be "very good"—valuable and worth caring for—and his plans for the future include its restoration (Romans 8:19–22). Being a friend of God involves viewing the world the same way he does.

A promising feature of Christianity here is its frontal assault on selfishness. The greedy self must be restrained first by justice, and then converted by grace. Its ravenous appetite for more is to be transformed by an infusion of love—the power of self-forgetful giving, rooted in a valuation of the other. Scripture teaches us not to spend everything on ourselves. We are to hold the created order in trust, especially for future generations.

Creation is an ever-present witness to the reality and wonder of God. Avery Dulles arrived at Harvard University in 1936 as an agnostic. One gray February day he took a break from his studies in the library. He describes that moment in his memoir:

> I was irresistibly prompted to go out into the open air.... The
> slush of melting snow formed a deep mud along the banks of
> the River Charles, which I followed down toward Boston....
> As I wandered aimlessly, something impelled me to look con-
> templatively at a young tree. On its frail, supple branches were
> young buds.... While my eye rested on them, the thought
> came to me suddenly, with all the strength and novelty of a
> revelation, that these little buds in their innocence and meek-
> ness followed a rule, a law of which I as yet knew nothing....
> That night, for the first time in years, I prayed.[10]

His testimony reminds us of the revelatory power of nature. Its
witness must not be suppressed, but nurtured and sustained, for natural beauty is a window that opens out onto God.

Probably no Christian has modeled harmony with nature better
than Francis of Assisi. Like Jesus himself, he practiced a love for God
so lavish that it spilled even beyond humanity to encompass everything the Creator had brought into being. Perhaps we touch Francis's
spirit most closely in his *Canticle of Brother Sun*, which reads in part:

> Praised be my Lord God for all his creatures, especially for
> our brother the sun ... for our sister the moon, and for the
> stars ... for our brother the wind ... for our sister water ...
> for our brother fire.... Praised be my Lord for our mother the
> earth, who sustains us and keeps us and brings forth various
> fruits and flowers of many colors, and grass.

Francis uses the language of interdependent family. This is not
pantheism or nature worship. It speaks, rather, of a relational intimacy
with nature—an enjoyment of, and respect for, it—that can and
should flourish within the larger, sanctifying orb of friendship with
God the creator of all.

Fifteen hundred years ago Benedict, the hermit-cum-monk,
pointed Christians in the right direction when he figured out that our
relationship with God has implications for how we relate to others.

This insight was extended even further by Francis to encompass our relationship to the created order. Together, their perceptions point to an overarching truth of the spiritual life—that our relationship with God will leave some marks on us. Inevitably we will be changed by it. In the next two chapters we will consider some other transformational consequences of Christ being with us and in us.

SOME HELPFUL GUIDES

BENEDICT (480 – 550 AD)

As a pioneer of the Christian monastic tradition, Benedict developed the communal dimension of Christian spirituality. His insights were enshrined in the influential *Rule of St. Benedict* (ca 525 AD). Reacting against the extreme individualism of the Desert Fathers, Benedict saw communal dynamics of obedience, forbearance, tolerance, and forgiveness as important (even indispensable) for soul-crafting.

DIETRICH BONHOEFFER (1906 – 1945)

Bonhoeffer was a brilliant young German Lutheran of the earlier twentieth century. He stood for the spiritual independence of the church, and took an active role in the underground resistance to Adolf Hitler's government. His opposition to the established order eventually cost him his life. Bonhoeffer portrayed Jesus Christ as "the-man-for-others." His *Life Together*, a brief but profound vision of Christian community, has become a modern classic.

MIROSLAV VOLF

Miroslav Volf is a professor of theology at Yale Divinity School, and a leading evangelical thinker today. A native of Croatia, he writes out of his own poignant firsthand experience of ethnic violence during the tragic war in former Yugoslavia. Sensitive to the dynamics of alienation and hatred, he calls the church to be a reconciled and reconciling community. His book *Exclusion and Embrace* has received wide acclaim, and *Free of Charge* explores giving and forgiving in a culture stripped of grace.

CHAPTER SUMMARY

The first dynamic of Christian spirituality is relational. It involves friendship with God and the experience of community. In this chapter, we considered our horizontal relationships with others and creation. The self-giving love of God contagiously infects all those who draw close to him. They begin a regenerated journey that leads beyond self-absorption to welcoming others. They joyfully participate in the expanding web of relationships that grace makes possible. This divine uniting impulse, which the church is called to model, should also lead to a harmonious relationship with creation.

PART 2

THE TRANSFORMATIONAL DYNAMIC: CHRIST *IN* US

We were created holy and whole,
but our sin has damaged us.
By his Spirit, Christ is purifying
and healing our true selves.

THE RENEWAL OF HOLINESS

Be holy because I, the LORD your God, am holy.

Leviticus 19:2

My wife and I spent the summer of 1981 in England, mostly at Cambridge. We lived in a friend's flat and got around on bicycles. We punted on the river Cam, ate hot fish and chips wrapped in newspaper, studied in the big library where they actually *brought* you the books, strolled college quadrangles, and meditated in chapels with dark, echoing ceilings. We sat where Milton wrote and where Charles Simeon preached, and prayed that a wee bit of their greatness might soak into us.

But we were curious to know what the *other* ancient English university was like. So one day, stretching our student budget to the max, we rented a Ford Escort and headed cross-country—along narrow roads, through tiny towns, and past countless pubs with quirky names—until we finally saw before us, through the trees, the luminous profusion of spires that is Oxford. One of my priorities was to visit Lincoln College, where John Wesley, founder of the Methodists, and his friends had studied on the eve of the Great Awakening.

The porter at the gate to the college saw us coming. As I stepped up to his window, he reached out and dangled an enormous iron key in my face. "Here it is," he said. "This is what you want. Now carry

on through. Take the first flight of stairs up to the right. And be sure
and return the key on your way out."

"But," I protested with some bewilderment, "I haven't even told
you why we've come."

"You didn't have to," he said with a dismissive wave of his hand.
"You're here to see where John Wesley stayed. You want to *behold*
where he and his fellow students held their meetings of the Holy
Club. That key you're holding in your hand will work just fine." We
climbed the stairs, unlocked the door, and entered the spartan little
room. I tried to visualize a young Wesley here, on his knees in prayer
with future giants like his brother Charles and their friend George
Whitefield, all of them imploring God for assistance in their pursuit
of personal holiness. Frankly, I found it incredible that college under-
graduates of *any* century would maintain a student organization with
a name like that.

Wesley's evangelical conversion occurred years later, at a chapel on
Aldersgate Street in London, where his heart was strangely warmed.
Years before that, the Holy Club had tapped into an established tradition of Anglican spirituality, a tradition freshly informed by William
Law and his *Serious Call to the Devout and Holy Life* (1728). Wesley's
interest in personal holiness did not diminish after his conversion. It
pervaded his passion for discipleship, for small groups, and personal
accountability. He urged all Methodists to pursue the narrow path to
Christian perfection.[1]

The pursuit of holiness became a defining feature of Methodist
spirituality, and helped shape postcolonial America. And it proved
to be the chief stimulus for the much broader, transdenominational
Holiness movement of the nineteenth century. Wesley represents an
important dynamic of Christian spirituality, one to which many others, including Ignatius Loyola and the Jesuits, John Bunyan and the
Puritans, and Hannah Whitall Smith and the Keswick movement,
have all contributed as well. It is a spiritual impulse that can be traced
back through the monastic traditions of Christian history to the Old
Testament book of Leviticus.

The Holiness of God

Holiness, the attribute of God most frequently announced in the Bible, means that God is separate and distinct from everything he has made, and separate too from even the slightest hint of sin or evil. There are no character flaws, impure motives, or wrongful behaviors in God, who dwells in shining, unapproachable light.

This truth brackets Scripture. The Old Testament prophet Isaiah declared, "Holy, holy, holy is the LORD Almighty" (Isaiah 6:3). His threefold repetition of the word "holy" was a Hebrew way of reinforcing the point—of declaring it impossible for God to be more holy than he is. In the last book of the New Testament, John's vision of the throne of God resonates perfectly. There angelic beings are proclaiming, day and night without a pause, "Holy, holy, holy is the Lord God Almighty" (Revelation 4:8).

And then, flowing out of this, there is an invitation and command to all God's people: "Be holy because I, the LORD your God, am holy" (Leviticus 19:2). This moral imperative stands firm as revelation progresses from the old covenant to the new. The apostle Peter confirms that it is still in force. "Do not conform to the evil desires you had when you lived in ignorance," he says. "But just as he who called you is holy, so be holy in all you do; for it is written: 'Be holy, because I am holy'" (1 Peter 1:14–16).

Often the pursuit of holiness is misconstrued as us doing God a favor. In reality, just the opposite is true. This is the path—the only one, really—to freedom from the toxins that pollute our lives, corrupt our characters, poison our memories, and ultimately make us hate ourselves. Sanctification, from the Latin *sanctus*, which means holy, refers to a lifelong process—the progressive renewal of holiness in the lives of believers. Such sanctification is actually God's gift, not something he imposes. It is his gracious way of satisfying our deep, soulful longing for what is good, true, and beautiful. When we grasp this, we are not so inclined to resist the purifying impulses of his Spirit.

Being in relationship with God begins our transformation. True friendship with him is always *transforming* friendship. It never leaves us unchanged. The apostle Paul explains this by an analogy to Moses on Mount Sinai, when God gave the Ten Commandments. "We all, who with unveiled faces contemplate the Lord's glory," he explains, "are being transformed into his image with ever-increasing glory" (2 Corinthians 3:18). It is a matter of reflected glory.

THE GOAL OF CHRISTLIKENESS

For Christians, the ultimate goal of sanctification is Christlikeness. The apostle Paul wrote: "For those God foreknew he also predestined to be conformed to the image of his Son, that he might be the firstborn among many brothers and sisters" (Romans 8:29). It is God's purpose that the character of Jesus Christ will be replicated many times over among those who follow him.

The goal, then, toward which human transformation properly moves, is enshrined not only in written guidelines and lofty ethical ideals. Perfection has been embodied in a historical person — the Holy One. Jesus Christ became the prototype and model of a brand-new line of humanity. Paul described him as the *second* Adam — human character in a whole new mold.

Meditation on the Gospel portrayals of Christ can be very profitable. Moreover, the Holy Spirit, who is also "the Spirit of Christ" (Romans 8:9), can help us become more faithful to the timeless likeness of Christ. The fruit of the Spirit (Galatians 5) is a rather striking portrait of Jesus as described in the New Testament. And it is this portrait the Spirit seeks to replicate in the lives of believers in every culture and epoch.

Holiness is an impulse of God's Spirit. The Nicene Creed of 381 AD pointedly affirms the divinity of the Spirit of God by describing him as "the Lord and giver of life." Since the Spirit is divine, it should come as no surprise to anyone that his most frequently used designation in the Bible is "the *Holy* Spirit." While many characteristics of the Spirit are revealed in Scripture, only one gets embedded in his very name. Obviously it is an important one. It is a reminder that we cannot become intimate with the Holy Spirit while stubbornly harboring evil in our heart. It reminds us that holiness is always high on the Spirit's agenda — and chiefly for our benefit, not his.

THE PERVERSITY RUNS DEEP

But we are divine image-bearers who sin. There is no denying the sin factor. We are *not* holy. Our natures are strangely perverse, and the perversity runs deep.

Imagine for a moment that it is garbage collection day in your community. You're carrying your cans out to the curb for morning pickup. Your neighbor across the street—let's call him Phil—is doing the same thing. Coming over, he says: "Guess what? I just won the lottery! Who would have thought I'd be a multimillionaire? But it nets out to this. I don't have to work another day in my life. And the missus and I have decided for starters to move up to a bigger place."

Many emotions flood your consciousness. But you manage, barely, to conceal them. Through gritted teeth and a phony smile, you respond as social protocol demands. "That's great, Phil," you say. "I'm really happy for you." Inside you know that Phil has just ruined your day.

You turn to go, but as you do your neighbor interrupts: "There's just one other thing I need to let you know. My wife just got back some tests from the cancer clinic, and I'm afraid it doesn't look good at all. She tested positive, and worse than that, it's already spread pretty far. Not much they can do now, they say. It's just a matter of time."

You have social skills. You know what must be said. "Oh Phil, that's horrible news. I'm so sorry for you. Let us know if we can do anything." You shake hands and part. But as you retrace your steps up the driveway, you are vaguely aware that you are feeling quite a bit better already. The last piece of news has put you in a much better frame of mind.[2] Innocuous self-interest bleeds so smoothly into malice. Most of us can identify. The inner moral territory is all too familiar. The story illustrates why the transformation of our souls is both necessary and difficult.

Most of the evil in the world originates from inside us, which is why Jesus taught that we need to be changed from the inside out. It also explains why classic Christian spirituality took the challenge of the sinful nature so seriously, practiced self-examination, cultivated virtue, and embraced spiritual disciplines. The goal has always been the transformation of the heart—the inner command-center of a person's being.

THE CHALLENGE OF CHANGE

Real change *is* possible, but it is always very, very difficult. If anyone doubts this, they should simply try to lose some weight and keep it off. In their *Westminster Confession of Faith* (1647), a group of prominent Puritans affirmed that Christians should expect to grow in godliness. But they did so very cautiously. Sanctification, they wrote, is "imperfect in this life; there abide still some remnants of corruption in every part: whence arises a continual and irreconcilable war; the flesh lusting against the Spirit, and the Spirit against the flesh." Perhaps they were just being honest. Other groups of Christians, however, like the Methodists and their Holiness successors, have considered this statement insufficiently optimistic—effectively a counsel of despair. Yet assurances from the other side that perfection (or, entire sanctification) is well within reach of all sincere Christians has never carried the day either. Similar skepticism greets the triumphant rhetoric of those who promise soaring moral flight high above all temptation and failure, simply by "reckoning" ourselves dead to sin and alive to Christ.

We have to be careful to strike the right balance. Real and lasting transformation is possible but difficult. It is possible because the Spirit is alive in us. It is difficult because the "cement" of our character hardens fairly early on in life. The default settings of our psyches, the grooves in which our thoughts run, get worn into place with the years. From a human development perspective, "formation" is best reserved for children. When it comes to adults, the progress of sanctification is largely a work of *re*-formation. Moreover, significant change tends to require supernatural help from beyond ourselves. We are rightly thrilled by tales of dramatic, instantaneous transformations. Sometimes this is the way grace comes to us. But most often transformation takes time. And it starts with being honest about our true condition.

PRISONERS IN CANADA

My good friend Gary and his brother Donnie grew up in a troubled family in a poor, crime-ridden neighborhood. Their older brother had been murdered point-blank by a shotgun blast through the screen door at the front of their house. Donnie had been in and out of jail for years on a list of criminal convictions. His last felony, for kidnapping and extortion, had brought a lengthy sentence behind bars.

When my wife and I were about to move to British Columbia, quite close to where Donnie was imprisoned, Gary asked me to consider visiting his brother in jail. That began a season of Sunday afternoon visits to the penitentiary up the valley. As we sat together in the snack area of the prison, or walked around the grounds in the afternoon sunshine, I learned that my friend's brother was actually not guilty of the crime for which he had been charged. He explained how he had been set up by unscrupulous friends who were still at large; he had been a victim of overzealous cops and an incompetent judiciary.

This was all surprising enough, but as I met other inmates I made an even more amazing discovery. None of them was really to blame for the crimes they were accused of having perpetrated. If I could believe what I was hearing, the prison was full of innocent people. It was very disillusioning: How could the Canadian legal system have become so totally messed up?

The inmates were in denial. But those inmates were not the only ones. We all are. God is a God of truth, and he refuses to play games. Teresa of Avila, the sixteenth-century Spanish mystic, may have been the originator of the insight that the journey to God is also "a journey to the self, a movement into self-knowledge."[3] As sinners, we tend to be out of touch with our true selves. It is too painful, too terrifying, to be honest about what is actually there. Only when we have first grasped God's assurance through Christ of unconditional love and forgiveness—the hope that we will be accepted *anyway*—can we find the courage to face the truth about ourselves. Honesty always grows best where grace is celebrated.

THE IMPORTANCE OF AUTHENTICITY

When I go to the dentist, he puts a little bib on me and leans me way back in his big chair. He tells me to open my mouth real wide, and then he clicks on a powerful overhead lamp. On the monitor out the corner of my eye, I can see what he sees. It's embarrassing. My gums are exposed, and my teeth too, and they are far from perfect. Nothing is symmetrical. The light exposes how much cleaning I need, the plaque buildup here and there, the molars that have become discolored over the years, and the ones that need fillings or crowns. It's not a very pretty sight. But the bright light is necessary if the dentist is going to be able to assess my dental situation accurately. Assessment is the first step to treatment and correction.

Confession is important to conversion for the same reason. If we *confess* our sins, the Bible says, God is faithful and just and will forgive and purify us (1 John 1:9). The Greek word that we translate "confess" means to agree or concur—to say the same thing. So why is confession a nonnegotiable element in conversion and the ongoing process of sanctification? It is essential because we need to assent to God's bracingly accurate assessment of our hearts and minds. We have to stop playing games. We must drop our rationalizations and come clean. We need to *agree* with God in our hearts.

And sometimes—just sometimes, I think—the breakthrough to authenticity requires that we come out of our comfortable privacy and confess our sins to others (James 5:16). This is risky business, and we need to choose our confidants wisely. Agreeing with God's assessment *in public*—finally being honest before God and others—can be the thing that at last brings us into the light.

DASHING CHILDREN AGAINST THE ROCKS

Psalm 137 is one strange piece of work. It's one of the imprecatory Psalms, that troublesome category of prayers that call down curses on enemies. This one was written by a Jew in exile who was being psychologically tormented by his captors. He had been through so much—in all likelihood, he had witnessed firsthand Israel's cat-astrophic military defeat; had probably seen his own little children grabbed from the heels by laughing soldiers, whirled around like sling-shots, and bashed against a wall until their skulls were crushed. Now, years later, these same Babylonians mocked him. "Entertain us with songs of your homeland and that beloved capital city of yours," they taunted. Overcome with hatred and unresolved grief, the psalmist seethes under his breath: "Happy are those who repay you according to what you have done to us. Happy are those who seize *your* infants and dash them against the rocks" (Psalm 137:8–9).

This is definitely not turning the other cheek. This is raw hate. It is perplexing that such dark passions should be enshrined in the inspired prayer book of Jews and Christians. What is going on? The presence of these sentiments in Scripture, says Eugene Peterson, is not an endorsement of these emotions. The Bible is not saying that this is how we ought to respond to the pain inflicted on us. The commend-able thing about the psalmist's reaction is that he is willing to pray his pain. He is willing to bring his true feelings into the presence of God and to express them with shocking honesty. This is what he does right. By bringing this pain and anger into the presence of God, the psalmist is bringing it into the only place that offers hope of dealing with it.[4] Real spirituality is always earthy and honest.

There is a danger that the pursuit of holiness can become theatri-cal. It is tempting to play to our audiences. We feed off the approval of others. But Jesus himself had little patience with cosmetic holiness. He didn't like it when people tooted their own horns. For example, it was better, he said, for people who were fasting to act normal and upbeat, instead of drawing attention to their superior piety through groans and other posturing.

He despised phoniness. "Woe to you, teachers of the law and Pharisees, you hypocrites! You clean the outside of the cup and dish, but inside they are full of greed and self-indulgence" (Matthew 23:25). For Jesus, that kind of discrepancy was untenable. He preferred a chronic sinner with heartfelt remorse to a religious leader puffed up by his own attainments.

THE DEATH OF THE OLD NATURE

Once we are able to face our own moral pathology honestly, what can we do about it? The apostle Paul expressed the inward struggle that every sensitive conscience experiences between their higher ideals and their lower compulsions. "Although I want to do good, evil is right there with me. For in my inner being I delight in God's law; but I see another law at work in me, waging war against the law of my mind and making me a prisoner of the law of sin at work within me. What a wretched man I am! Who will rescue me from this body of death?" (Romans 7:21–24). Even after regeneration, it seems, the old nature keeps coming back to haunt us.

Fortunately, Paul saw hope of relief. "Thanks be to God," he wrote a sentence later, "who delivers me through Jesus Christ our Lord!" (7:25). The renewal of holiness is God's work accomplished through the indwelling Spirit of Christ. No self-improvement strategy can void our need for this help from beyond ourselves. Once we understand this, we can start to cooperate with the impulses of the Holy Spirit operating inside us. We can throw ourselves more enthusiastically in line with the direction God wants to move. We can exercise our power of choice to accelerate the rate of transformation in our lives.

It starts by changing how we think of ourselves. Since the inception of Christianity, water baptism has been the mandatory rite of initiation into the Christian community. It was understood, by Christians and non-Christians alike, to mark the end of one's old allegiances and the inauguration of a new life as a committed follower of Jesus Christ. It was (pardon the pun) the watershed moment in one's spiritual journey back to God.

Paul recommended a radical view of the baptismal experience. He taught that we should consider it a funeral service for our sinful natures. "All of us who were baptized into Christ Jesus were baptized into his death[.] We were therefore buried with him through baptism into death in order that, just as Christ was raised from the dead through the glory of the Father, we too may live a new life" (Romans 6:3–4). In effect, Paul was recommending a special visualization technique. When we recall our baptism, he was saying, we are to think of ourselves as having *joined* Christ in his experience of death and resurrection.

Elsewhere the apostle conjures up the memory of Isaac, tied to a mountaintop altar of sacrifice, while his wild-eyed father Abraham stands over him with a knife of execution held high. "Offer *your* bodies as a living sacrifice, holy and pleasing to God" (Romans 12:1), Paul urges. This is radical, bracing—offensive, even. Burials, deaths, and human sacrifices—it's creepy stuff. Is it necessary? Is it even healthy? And in Galatians it comes up again: "I have been crucified with Christ," the apostle says, "and I no longer live, but Christ lives in me" (Galatians 2:20). The main point is: in the act of dying something in us falls away. It comes to a decisive end in a way only possible through dying. And Paul teaches that this is how we ought to regard our old nature and its persistent demands for unholy satisfaction.

On a hillside overlooking the ancient city of Ephesus are the ruins of the massive Church of St. John, constructed on the order of Emperor Justinian and thought to hold beneath its altar the bones of the beloved apostle. The remains of this once-great church, now sadly exposed to open air and the elements, contain a fascinating baptistery, built in the shape of a cross, into which each candidate would descend along the central channel. Even the room housing the baptistery was cruciform in shape. What a powerful architectural witness to the New Testament understanding of baptism as a symbolic identification with Christ in death to self and resurrection to new life.

DISCIPLINING THE SELF

Still, the unholy compulsions of our sinful nature never stop making themselves felt in our hearts. Its appetites remain strong. That's why it has to be continually reined in. That's why firm discipline of the self is so important to the Christian life.

I was on a church platform during an ordination service on a hot Saturday afternoon. The charge to the candidate was inordinately long and prosaic, and my mind began to wander. I noticed that there were four stained-glass windows on each side of the sanctuary, each representing a fruit of the Spirit. Down one side, in Gothic script and the language of the old King James Bible, were the words *love, joy, peace,* and *long-suffering.* Down the other side were *gentleness, goodness, faith,* and *meekness.*

I knew there was one more fruit. So where was the ninth? I looked up toward the balcony and all around, searching for a final window to complete the inspired text. It didn't exist. In the architect's mind, the symmetry of eight, an even number, had trumped the need to complete the biblical text. I concluded with some alarm that perhaps this church did not believe in *self-control.*

We ought to believe in its necessity (as I'm sure the church in question did as well). There is a strand of thinking among some Protestants that intentional self-discipline for the purposes of holiness smacks of "works" — that great enemy of salvation by grace alone through faith alone. The catechism of the Roman Catholic Church says that "the way of perfection passes by way of the cross. There is no holiness without renunciation and spiritual battle." Biblically informed Christians should have no problem with the basic idea here. God is engaged in soul-crafting and the formation of virtue in us.[5] It is his work, yet it is a process in which we are invited to participate — by responding in a willing, cooperative way to the impulses of the Holy Spirit.

This seems to be how the apostle Paul, who knew a thing or two about salvation by grace through faith, understood life in the Spirit. *"Clothe yourselves* with the Lord Jesus Christ, and do not think about how to gratify the desires of the sinful nature," he wrote to the Romans (Romans 13:14). *"Set your minds* on things above, not on earthly things," he urged the Colossians. "For you died, and your life is now hidden with Christ in God" (Colossians 3:2–3). Immediately afterward he added, in the same epistle, *"Put to death,* therefore, whatever belongs to your earthly nature" (3:5). I have highlighted in italics the specific commands involved. It certainly sounds as though we are being asked to do things that will assist the sanctification process.

Christians have debated — often vigorously — whether the pursuit of holiness is optional or mandatory for their salvation. It is really an unhelpful way to frame the issue. It is much better to say that growth in holiness is *natural* and inevitable for regenerate believers — because it expresses their new spiritual DNA. Martin Luther, the great Reformer, held firm that Christians are justified by faith in Christ alone, apart from works of the law. But then he added that once a person is justified, they cannot and will not remain idle. For they now have the Spirit, "and where the Holy Ghost dwells, he will not suffer a man to be idle, but stirs him up to all exercise of piety and godliness."[6] We can choose to align ourselves with these divine impulses — giving ourselves to them with all our heart. This involves an acquired taste for the good revealed in Christ, a genuine delight in the holy, and a realization that this Spirit-guided process is the key to reclaiming our true selves.

⸰ SOME HELPFUL GUIDES ⸰

THOMAS À KEMPIS (CA 1380 – 1471)

Thomas à Kempis was a member of the Brothers and Sisters of the Common Life in the Netherlands. His example of meditation on the inner life of Christ contributed to a spiritual renewal movement in his day. For over five hundred years his *Imitation of Christ* (first version, 1429), to which some coauthors may also have contributed, has been the unchallenged masterpiece of Christian devotional literature and the imitative tradition. Casual contemporary readers may find its intensity to be daunting.

HANNAH WHITALL SMITH (1832 – 1911)

Hannah Whitall Smith, a Quaker from Philadelphia, was a leader of the late nineteenth-century "Higher Christian Life" movement, which extended the influence of Holiness themes throughout Protestant life, and also helped stimulate and sustain robust missionary initiatives globally. Her popular-level and bestselling *The Christian's Secret of a Happy Life* (1875) offered an upbeat corrective to the cheerless introspection some believed had too often characterized the pursuit of holiness.

J. I. PACKER

J. I. Packer, author of *Knowing God*, has been described as "the last of the Puritans." A British Anglican theologian who came to Canada in the 1970s, Packer has been an important mediator to the contemporary church of the spiritual vision of the seventeenth-century Puritans and their descendents in early America. Packer's own appropriation of this tradition may be studied in such works as *Keeping in Step with the Spirit* and *Rediscovering Holiness*.

CHAPTER SUMMARY

We began our consideration of the transformational dynamic by studying the renewal of holiness. Sin has corrupted the moral purity of people created in the holy God's image and likeness. We have become image-bearers *who sin*, and worse than that, we carry about in us a disposition to sin. The gospel is the good news that our sinful thoughts and actions can be forgiven through the atoning work of Christ. But the news is even better than this. God's Spirit, who now resides in us, is also fixing the polluted source of our sins. He is gently but firmly moving us along in the direction of sanctification, progressively restoring the holiness with which we were originally designed.

5

THE HEALING OF
OUR WOUNDS

I am the LORD, who heals you.
Exodus 15:26

It was my first day ever in the Borneo jungle, and I had been look-ing forward to the adventure for a long time. Two Christian tribal leaders, John and Nelson, agreed to be my guides on a demanding (well, for me anyway) trek to the famous Nian caves outside of Miri. The jungle was like a sauna under the canopy of towering green growth, and before long I was totally wet—soaked right through—with my own perspiration. Even the dollar bills in my wallet were sopping. We saw amazing ironwood trees with huge, naturally but-tressed trunks that challenge the sharpest chainsaws. Along the way we passed through a village with a double longhouse that was home for about eighty families. On the edge of this town, under a roof of stained corrugated metal, was a tiny shrine to the invisible spirits—a clear indication that the community was still animist.

Further down the trail a bird flew across our path, and that got my tribal friends talking about the old days. Back then, they said, a hummingbird crossing in front of you was an evil omen. The spirits were telling you to turn back on pain of death. Your journey, regard-less of its urgency, had to be aborted. Likewise, if a hummingbird flew past your longhouse window in the morning, you dared not go out that day, and had to hunker down at home. No one had the courage to defy these fearsome taboos. It struck me as so twisted that such a delicate and wondrous little aviator should have become, in the superstitious minds of the people, a symbol of terror.

But in the 1930s the gospel came to the alcohol-ravaged headhunters of this region, and after the interlude of the Japanese occupation in the early 1940s, flourished here in this remote part of Malaysia. The tribal peoples — Ibans and others — were drawn in great numbers to the message of Christ's superior power over all the foreboding supernatural forces in their world. Today the grandchildren of those first converts drive around in Isuzu Troopers, attend beautiful churches, and work in the highest professions. But I tried to imagine what it must have been like for that *first* Christian believer, dressed in a simple loincloth, to be out on a trail like ours and have a hummingbird whir by. It must have required enormous courage, and with his heart no doubt pounding, to take that very first and unprecedented step ahead along the path. But in doing so, he was wrenching himself, and those he inspired, free from the old paradigm of fear. In taking that step forward rather than back, they began to experience divine healing of their long-terrorized minds and souls.

In the previous chapter we began our consideration of the transformational dynamic of Christian spirituality by studying the renewal of holiness. This is crucial, but God's intentions for us are not restricted to sanctification. His saving plan is to change us into persons who are both holy and *whole*. This chapter continues to explore spiritual transformation by focusing on the movement of the Spirit toward the healing of our wounds.

SOURCES OF OUR WOUNDS

Sin, whether our own or someone else's, is never good for us. It always ends up causing pain and suffering, and its negative impact on our emotional lives can be huge. It tends to weaken us and diminish our ability to do the right thing in difficult circumstances, takes a toll on our sense of self, and robs us of the best experiences in life.

Our wounding comes mainly from three sources: our own sinful behaviors, the sinful behaviors of others, and the realities of a fallen world. No one needs reminding that we regularly hurt ourselves through our own bad, selfish, impulsive, rebellious decisions. We pay dearly for these choices. Advertisers in the marketplace often suggest that sinning is "cool" and fun, but this may be the ultimate lie. In the end, the Bible warns, sinning turns bitter and leads to death (Proverbs 5:3–5; Romans 6:23). Onlookers may feel sympathetic about the horrible mess we have gotten ourselves into, and certainly God cares about our plight. But this does not change the fact that we are still to blame.

Yet we carry other wounds that were not self-inflicted. We have all been hurt by the sinful, insensitive, or clumsy behaviors of other people. Individuals and groups have wounded me in ways I did not deserve, and likewise there are innocent people who have been victimized by my sinful behaviors. These scenarios continue all the time.

And finally, there are those wounds we acquire simply because we live in a fallen and dangerous world. Tsunami waves batter shorelines; earthquakes rock different parts of the planet — thousands of innocent people are killed and injured. These natural disasters, products of a world that is not right, are not invented or sent by human beings. The same explanation accounts for those who suffer from genetic defects, diseases, and the like.

Naming these three sources is important because it underscores the important truth that those who suffer are only sometimes personally responsible for their own wounded condition. One of the cruelest things of all is to blame innocent victims for their own suffering. Such cruel reasoning was followed by the disciples of Jesus as they walked past a man suffering from congenital blindness. "Who sinned," they asked, "this man or his parents, that he was born blind?" (John 9:2). We can see that according to their worldview, there were only two possible explanations; it had to be one or the other. They assumed that a karmalike law of personal responsibility fully accounted for any tragedy that came up. But Jesus set the record straight.

Some readers will wonder if I should have listed a fourth source of wounding, namely, the Devil and his demons. After all, the Scriptures describe the Devil as an enemy who "prowls around like a roaring lion looking for someone to devour" (1 Peter 5:8). I do not deny the existence of this prowling opportunist, nor minimize his negative influence on the human condition. But I also want to be informed by Paul's exhortation that we are not to give the Devil any kind of foothold in our lives (Ephesians 4:27). This language suggests that the Devil most often prefers to exploit the existing variables we have just presented. Effective healing of humanity's wounds, therefore, cannot minimize or skip over these *direct* causes of suffering.[1]

THE SHAPE OF OUR WOUNDS

The wounds we acquire in the course of simply living our lives have many forms. It is painful just to think about them. They include traumatic memories, living with a disability, genetic disorders, mental illness, the dark cloud of depression, psychological fragility, damaged emotions, diseases, chronic pain, life regrets, confused sexual identity, and an uncertain sense of self—to name just a few. The scope of all this pain is staggering. There are so many ways in which we are not well. The following are just some easily recognized samples from a very long list.

We start with *bondages*. When we deliberately choose to engage in sinful acts, we may be startled to discover that our sins are *addictive* and we cannot break free from such behavior patterns, even when we try. We are slaves to things that we have actually grown to hate. Addiction to drugs is just one example of this. But it is also true of pornography, gambling, lying, and all sorts of other unhealthy behaviors that we gradually get hooked on.

Then there are our *fears*. Wounds inflicted upon us, especially during our childhoods, or by those closest to us, leave lasting psychological scars. If they are serious enough, they leave us with deep-seated fears that affect in very serious ways our ability to function in life and relationships. They can mean that we will behave irrationally in certain circumstances, unable to overcome the powerful impulses of our subconscious. These things can make us anxious and unsettled, never quite feeling at peace—always *agitated* about something. Sometimes they keep us from taking the risk of opening ourselves up to love and be loved. And as a consequence we remain profoundly lonely and incomplete—alone in the world.

Self-loathing is another common kind of wound. There is a price to be paid for willful sinning and going against the inner voice of conscience. This built-in moral monitor can afterward condemn us—reminding us that what we did was wrong and despicable (Romans 2:15). This can contribute to strong feelings of shame and self-loathing, so that we actually grow to hate ourselves. Our self-esteem plunges down, and we lose the confidence to step out in adventures with God.

What is even sadder is when people experience the wounds of shame and low self-esteem because *others* (parents, teachers, employers, spouses) have treated them cruelly and without love. Having internalized the negative assessments of others, they come to believe that they really are worthless creatures. This can produce all kinds of reckless behaviors—after all, who cares anyway?—that in the long run compound a hurting person's pain.

Sometimes the wounding goes so deep that we cannot find it within ourselves to *forgive* those who have injured us. We can't release them from what we see as their unfulfilled obligation to us, so the unresolved issue festers inside us. I think it was Anne Lamott who commented in her book *Traveling Mercies* that an inability to forgive is like drinking rat poison to exterminate the rodents on your property. The victim who is unable to forgive becomes doubly injured, for their inward feelings continue to damage their souls while the perpetrator moves on, blissfully untouched. For all these reasons, *and many others*, we are like the man in Jesus' parable who went down to Jericho, was assaulted by thieves and left for dead, beaten and bloodied on the roadside. We too need a Good Samaritan to come by and notice us.

THE GOD WHO HEALS

Recently I had the wonderful experience of attending the centennial celebration of the 1906 Azusa Street revival in Los Angeles. A friend and I drove up from San Diego to the Los Angeles Convention Center, where thousands of Pentecostals and charismatic believers from around the world were honoring the roots of their moment— one that has already grown globally to over six hundred million persons. We also visited the tiny Bonnie Brae House, where Pentecostal pioneer William Seymour and others had their first experience of Spirit-baptism accompanied by tongues; and later, the massive Angelus Temple, founded in the 1920s by dramatic Foursquare Gospel leader Aimee Semple McPherson. It was a great day.

Among other things, I was looking forward to hearing the renowned Roman Catholic charismatic Francis McNutt speak on, and pray for, divine healing. As I approached the huge auditorium, the hallways became clogged with people, even though it was some time before McNutt's scheduled address. The auditorium, we discovered, was already so packed—every square foot of floor space occupied— that security guards had been called to bring order and forcibly close the doors on the outstretched arms of the excluded. There was ample seating in adjacent sessions on theology, I noted ruefully, but it was clear that the greater heart cry of the people was for God's healing touch. It has always been so, but never more than in our own day when pain is so pervasive and raw.

God delivers us from the guilt of sin. As our sanctifier, he progressively sanctifies us and makes us holy. But this is not the whole story. He is also our *Healer*, because he doesn't want us to continue to live with the wounds that sin has caused in our experiences of life. This is one of the great titles for God in the Old Testament: "I am the LORD, who heals you" (Exodus 15:26).

We will remember how central the ministry of healing was in the earthly life of Jesus (Matthew 4:23–24; Acts 10:38). It was a response of *compassion* to the suffering he saw, and the compassion *moved* him (Matthew 9:36, King James Version) to do something about it. It is equally noteworthy that the apostles continued this healing ministry after Christ's ascension. Healing is a powerful and pervasive biblical motif. It means that God's salvation plan is comprehensive enough to address both the guilt and the *consequences* of sin in the world.

God's Grace as Mending Glue

I take heart whenever I see Warren in the seminary hallways. About a decade ago he was a cocaine addict and drug dealer with a failing marriage. But the Healer got to him, and the old is being transformed. With his wife he now leads a church he planted in his hometown in the desert, and on the side he has a respected community ministry to drug addicts.

When I go over to the Starbucks a block away from campus, I often see Rick there with his newspaper. He's retired now, and serves as an usher in his church on Sundays. He was a down-and-out alcoholic, but he's content now to sip coffee. He can't replace the years the locusts ate, but there's a tenderness in his eyes that says he's still amazed by the Healer's touch.

I know someone who was told she was worthless all her life, and kicked out of her house by a raging parent who hated her. By the healing grace of God, today she is a graciously confident woman who cares deeply for others in pain.

None of these people has it all together yet, but they know something of what Eugene O'Neill meant when he said: "Man is born broken. He lives by mending. The grace of God is the glue."[2]

The healing process begins the moment we enter into a saving relationship with God through Jesus Christ and receive his renewing Holy Spirit into our hearts. The touching of our pain, and the recovery from our soul injuries, is launched right then and there. This is the natural starting point for what the great theologian Francis Schaeffer called "the substantial healing of the total person."[3] Schaeffer referred to it, however, as the *substantial*, not the complete, healing of the individual. What we can experience is real and significant healing, but it is never quite complete or total on this side of eternity. That's what we mean when we say that God's healing of believers is "already" (in part) but still "not yet" (in totality).

Even though many Christians testify gratefully to God's healing touch on their bodies, every one of us continues to age, and eventually will die. The effects of sin on our mortality are not completely overcome—for that, we must wait for the resurrection of the body. Similarly with our psychological and emotional wounds, we look forward to the day when we will be glorified and our residual scars will all be made completely whole. This is certainly what the apostle John had in mind about heaven when he described a river of life flowing from the throne of God. The river irrigates the tree of life, whose leaves "are for the healing of the nations" (Revelation 22:2).

Physical Healing

God wants to see us healed in every dimension of ourselves—both physically and psychologically. Throughout history Christians have earnestly desired to experience the healing touch of God for our *physical* problems and wounds. The book of James encourages believers to pray for healing, and when appropriate to gather the elders and be anointed with oil to symbolize our desire for the Healer's touch (James 5:14–16).

One of the most famous of all Christian pilgrimage sites is Lourdes in southern France. For centuries people desperate for healing have traveled to this place to experience God's intervention. Some of them have left with joy, convinced that God dramatically answered their prayers while there. Abandoned crutches and wheelchairs are physical testimonies to their experiences, and sources of hope to others. Saint Joseph's Oratory in Montreal, Canada is a similar site. There the pickled heart of a devout monk, Brother André, serves as an object of devotion and hope for cure. The familiar apparatus of joyfully abandoned medical equipment is littered about, though on a smaller scale than at Lourdes. As moderns, we walk away confused about how much, if any, of these testimonials are credible and witness to facts. We despise gullibility and at the same time fear our own unbelief.

In the latter part of the nineteenth century, there was a surge of Protestant interest in supernatural "divine healing." Johann Blumhardt from Germany; Charles Cullis, a Boston physician; A. J. Gordon, the founder of what has become Gordon-Conwell Seminary in Massachusetts; and A. B. Simpson, the ex-Presbyterian founder of the Christian and Missionary Alliance, were in the vanguard of this so-called faith healing movement. Remarkable testimonies flowed out of this tradition. The operations of its "homes for healing" suggest to the credit of its early leaders that they tended to have a rather holistic understanding of healing.

At the same time the movement's participants had a decided preference for supernatural healing over normal medical treatment—in part because of the ammunition that it provided in their ideological contest against the sneering advocates of naturalism. The healing work of Christ was enshrined in the doctrinal statements of numerous Holiness and Pentecostal groups, and is regularly sought and celebrated in many of their assemblies.

Some Christians today believe that the special gifts of healing described in the New Testament (1 Corinthians 12:9, 28, for example) are no longer in operation, and therefore God no longer calls specific individuals to be healers in some special sense. Charismatic Christians disagree—they are convinced that such gifts *are* still in operation, and they cite high-profile figures like Kathryn Kuhlman (whom *Time* magazine once referred to as "a one-woman shrine of Lourdes") and Oral Roberts as examples.[4] Despite this difference of opinion about a continuing *gift* of healing, both groups of Christians agree that God still heals people through the believing prayers of his people. Today, especially in regions of the world where poverty abounds, and medical attention is inadequate, physical healing is one of the great blessings that believers find in their faith in Christ.

PHYSICIAN IN THE DESERT

Antony lived and prayed in the harsh Egyptian desert in the fourth century. Over the years his reputation for saintliness grew noteworthy. People traveled great distances from the comfortable urban centers of Rome's empire to witness this strange, otherworldly man of God, to solicit his wisdom and seek his healing touch. He had an enormous influence in his time.

Antony was regarded as a formidable spiritual warrior against the unseen forces of evil. He was also viewed as a person with gifts of healing and great discernment. These latter qualities are evident in a story told by his ancient biographer and architect of the Nicene Creed, Athanasius of Alexandria. On one occasion a man named Fronto traveled out to see Antony, the Desert Father, in the hope that he might be healed of various physical problems from which he suffered a great deal.[5]

But, as Richard Foster interprets the story,[6] Antony detected early on that this new disciple's devotion to him involved an unhealthy dependence. He saw a need for psychological wholeness as well as physical health, and recognized that in this case they were linked. And so, instead of immediately focusing on Fronto's physical needs, or moving directly to prayer and anointing with oil, Antony offered some unexpected advice. He challenged Fronto, in so many words, to take responsibility for his own life, and indicated that the man's physical healing would depend upon obediently taking this step. "Leave," he commanded, "and you will be healed."[7]

Fronto's neediness was evident in his excessive attachment to his master, and at first it was too powerful for him to overcome. He was not able to head off on his own. So he lingered, engaging in acts of service and devotion to this Desert Father whom he admired so much. For a while there was nothing Antony could do. The ailing disciple had a good heart but an underdeveloped self. For Fronto's own good, though, Antony kept trying, gently but firmly, to push him back into normal life with its adult demands. Otherwise the desert would only be a place of arrested development and escape.

Finally, as Foster summarizes the story, "in desperation over his physical illnesses and with great sadness, Fronto turned to leave his master. As he walked away, *he was healed.*"[8] That was the punch line. Antony's treatment plan was one that recognized the link between the physical and the psychological, and addressed them both together. After recounting numerous other healing stories of this nature, the great bishop and theologian Athanasius concludes his biography on Antony: "It was as if he were a physician given to Egypt by God."[9]

INNER HEALING[10]

Since the 1960s, at least in America and other industrialized nations with modern economies and higher standards of living, Christians have turned their attention from prayers for physical healing to quests for emotional or (as it is often called) "inner" healing. This is certainly an area in which God is also vitally interested. As the psalmist said, "He heals the brokenhearted and binds up their wounds" (Psalm 147:3). Brokenheartedness may have physical manifestations, but its roots are in the soul.

It may be that advanced medical knowledge and more accessible health care systems have made purely physical healings less of a priority for believers in more affluent countries. In any case, the focus has shifted to those wounds that medicine cannot so easily address — the *inner* wounds of the soul. It is in this area that the supernatural touch of the Healer is most intensely sought. This is an area where the newer charismatic movement has gravitated to a healing focus different from that of historic Pentecostalism. On both the Catholic and Protestant sides, the charismatic movement looks for ways to address the inner wounds of the soul.

One of the biggest obstacles to such "inner healing" is lack of self-awareness. Too often we are insufficiently in touch with our true selves to be more than vaguely aware of what is bothering us on the inside. Sometimes only through periods of solitude and silence, discerning mentors and soul-friends, and a newfound courage and willingness to *listen* to those who love us are we able to discern our wounds and then set about to receive God's healing for them.

PROVEN MEANS OF HEALING

It is a special evidence of the Spirit's gracious presence whenever healing occurs. Dramatic moments of instantaneous healing always receive the most press coverage, but we should not be blind to the much more frequent instances of quiet, progressive renewal and healing of damaged persons. Naturally our quest for wholeness cannot skirt the need in some instances for renewed holiness, and the repentance and renunciation this may require of us. But our primary concern here is those wounds which repentance cannot touch.

There are a number of proven means for the healing of these, and the first is the Word of God correctly interpreted. Within its inspired pages, we can discover the truth about both God and ourselves. So much of our pain stems from a false understanding of reality. We are the victims of imagined terrors, skewed perceptions, and misguided hopes. But "the life of the spirit," explained Thomas Merton, the Trappist monk from Kentucky, "by integrating us in the real order established by God, puts us in the fullest possible contact with reality—not as we imagine it, but as it really is."[11]

There is, then, a pastoral function to biblical truth. It renews our minds by helping us see things as they really are. For example, we are unable to get in touch with who we really are until we embrace God's estimate of us.[12] And that estimate is presented with clarity and authority in Scripture. We are transformed, as the apostle Paul said, by the renewing of our minds (Romans 12:2), and the Bible is the chief instrument of this renewal.

It is relatively easy to get our heads around the truths of Scripture. But the greater challenge is to get those truths to percolate down into the affective center of our being, where they can begin to alter the default settings of our psyches. This is where the classic disciplines of prayer, meditation, and contemplation (of which more will be said in a later chapter) come in. The wisdom of historic Christian spiritual practices is something we need to draw on as we seek to internalize the truths that can otherwise flit uselessly about in our brains.

A battle is going on in Christian circles over whether the Bible *alone* is sufficient to meet every challenge a counselor may face. Some insist it is, while others believe we are responsible to integrate the inspired teachings of Scripture with the best findings of psychological research and proven clinical techniques. I am convinced that the latter is the only responsible way to go. All truth is God's truth. Yes, it fills Scripture, but it is also found in many other places—including research journals. Just as the gentle hands of a surgeon help cure physical illness, so the discerning mind of a gifted therapist can be God's instrument for the healing of deep human pain.

As already noted, many of the wounds we have received have come from the hands of other human beings. These experiences have profoundly affected us. Like Floridians bracing for another hurricane, we tend to board up the doors and windows of our inner selves, so that we will not be injured again. We are more guarded and withdrawn in our relationships. Whether the victim of childhood abuse, an unfaithful marriage partner, an exploitative employer, or flagrant injustice in a Christian organization, we need somehow to have our trust in other people restored. The best means for reconstructing such trust is to encounter persons of integrity and compassion, and to be able to participate with them in circles of authentic community. This is an incredible opportunity for individual Christians, and also for church fellowships. There is a promising future for churches that are able and willing to be hospitals and hospices for souls.

Wounded Healers

Healing power can be found in service to others. The self-forgetfulness that service requires can itself be liberating, and the experience of making a difference in someone else's life can prove very encouraging and edifying for someone conscious of their own incompleteness. More will be said about service in later chapters on vocation, but here it leads very naturally to a consideration of what it means to be a wounded healer—a flawed but effective instrument of grace.

But can we *really* be of much use to wounded people unless all our own wounds are healed first? Henri Nouwen says we can. In fact, he suggests, an amazing paradox is in operation. Our own pain and continued wounds often lend an unexpected power and effectiveness to our efforts.[13]

This is a very encouraging suggestion. Upon reflection, it seems quite consistent with what the apostle Paul taught about the power of the Spirit being evident through "jars of clay" and those who were seemingly weak in themselves. This is a recurring theme in Paul's letter to those Corinthians who perceived themselves as strong and successful. From his own experience of an unidentified "thorn in the flesh," Paul knew that God's grace was sufficient, but also that his power was "made perfect in weakness" (2 Corinthians 4:7–12; 12:7–10).

So the good news is that usefulness need not be postponed until we finally have it all together. If it required that, we would never get around to ministry. God prefers to work through people who are not depending on their own competence or wellness, but on him working through them. We have come full circle to the theme of authenticity. Wounded people are drawn to those who speak honestly about themselves, and their limits, and do not pretend that they speak from a position of superiority, perfection, and competence. What is needed is not perfection, but a convincing testimony that there is hope of real, substantial healing. Perhaps our best hope lies in the promise of Psalm 126:6: "Those who go out weeping, carrying seed to sow, will return with songs of joy, carrying sheaves with them." In this confidence, the Spirit leads us into service—assuring us that Christ, who is already in us, will also work through us.

✑ Some Helpful Guides ✑

Antony of Egypt (251–356 AD)

Antony was the founder and most famous member of the early Christian ascetic movement known as the Desert Fathers and

Mothers. These individuals sought to escape the growing compromises of comfortable, legalized Christianity through retreat to the Egyptian desert for contemplation, spiritual warfare, and prayer. Antony is also remembered for a remarkable physical and inner healing ministry. His radical spirituality has been immortalized in *Life of Antony*, a biography by Athanasius.

HENRI NOUWEN (1932 – 1996)

Dutch-born Henri Nouwen ranked among the leading voices on Christian spirituality in the late twentieth century. His career encompassed a prestigious academic post at Harvard and residence in a community for persons with disabilities. His clinical psychology training gave his spirituality a profound therapeutic sensitivity and appeal. His special gifts were an intuitive awareness of the wounds of contemporary people and an ability to address those with a simplicity, depth, and hope focused on Christ. His many influential writings include *The Wounded Healer*, *Reaching Out*, and *The Return of the Prodigal Son*.

DAVID BENNER

Canadian David Benner, currently director of the Institute for Psychospiritual Health, has been a leading academic in the fields of psychology and counseling, and brought an informed Christian perspective to these fields. More recently his attention has become focused on the intersections between psychological health, pastoral care, and spiritual wellness. His works include *Sacred Companions*, *Healing Emotional Wounds*, and *The Gift of Being Yourself*.

CHAPTER SUMMARY

God's saving plan is to change us into persons who are both holy and whole. We have continued our study of the transformational dynamic by exploring the movement of the Spirit toward *wholeness*. The consequences of sin—whether ours or someone else's, it makes no difference—are painful and damaging. But God is the Great Physician—and out of compassion for us in our suffering, and by his Spirit, he has initiated a healing and restorative ministry in the world. It is substantial, though never complete, and it encompasses both our physical needs and our inner wounds. Pastors and Christian therapists often have important ministries in addressing this latter need. The encouraging news is that each of us can serve Christ as wounded healers of others.

PART 3

THE VOCATIONAL DYNAMIC: CHRIST *THROUGH* US

We were created for joyful participation in God's work
in the world, but sin has made our existence seem futile.
By his Spirit, Christ is rebuilding purpose
and meaning into our lives.

DISCOVERING PURPOSE AND MEANING

*"My food," said Jesus, "is to do the will of him
who sent me and to finish his work."*
John 4:34

Crowds of tourists with guidebooks and cameras continually pass through the ruins of Rome's ancient Forum. We were among them one day as we started out from the Colosseum and headed down past the Arch of Titus into the center of things. We passed derelict pagan temples, the chambers of the Senate, and the Mamertine Prison where the apostle Peter may have languished before his execution. And like everyone else, we eventually climbed back out and up to modern Capitol Hill at the north end with its regal statue of a mounted Marcus Aurelius.

This basin of rubble was once the epicenter of a sprawling empire. Clusters of toga-clad orators, lawyers, and generals laughed and whispered here. Caesars lived on the ridge, and vestal virgins stood between the columns of their temple at sunset. Laws were passed, military plans were approved, and the fates of millions were decided on this spot. But today grass grows over former imperial opulence, and fragments of marble columns litter the ground. The conditions testify that something catastrophic happened here. The disaster—at least the first phase of it—began in the early 400s with the barbaric invasions of once invincible Rome.

In the nearby Colosseum, Christians were once martyred as coarse entertainment for the pagan masses. But Christian fortunes eventually reversed with Emperor Constantine's change of heart. Just as the ark of the covenant once made the Philistines' inferior idol crash on the floor of its temple, so the cross, the Christians believed, had triumphed over the pantheon of Rome. From now on, they assumed, the advancement of their Savior's cause in the world would be intertwined with Rome's success.

The plundering of their great city shook the Roman Christians' worldview. They had invested heavily—too heavily, as it turned out—in a system now in collapse. Instead of blessing Rome, God appeared to have abandoned it. It made no sense that God would allow the Eternal City to be treated like this. The Christians were in shock and their faith in crisis. They had blithely assumed that history was advancing according to God's purposes, but now doubt reared its poisonous head. If God was not in control (and he appeared not to be), then perhaps history had no meaning after all. Could it be that the disciples of pagan Epicurus had been right: everyone should just eat, drink, and be merry, for tomorrow they would die?

For guidance the Christians turned to Augustine, one of their leaders who lived on the African side of the Mediterranean. "Help us make some sense out of everything that is happening," they pleaded, and Augustine responded by writing what became *The City of God*. It was a massive treatise offering the bewildered Christian community a meaning-making perspective on the catastrophic events they were experiencing. The most important thing Augustine did was assure them that history was still being directed by God. Things were not pointless and chaotic—they were unfolding beneath an intact canopy of meaning. Augustine's key idea was that there are actually *two* cities or communities under construction at any given time in the world— the City of Man and the City of God. The first is of the earth and dominated by love of self. The other is heavenly and characterized by love for God. One is doomed; the other is destined for glory.

The complicating factor is that these two cities are "interwoven, as it were, in this present transitory world, and mingled with one another."[1] As Augustine explained further, the City of God through the ages has been developing, "not in the light, but in the shadow."[2] Yet despite its obscurity, God's principal interest lies in the second great construction enterprise—and, unlike Rome, it is indestructible. Augustine's assurance to the Christians of his day, and his legacy to us, is that upheavals of human civilizations do not threaten the advance of God's agenda in the world. Despite the surface chaos that periodically engulfs us, there *is* a design and purpose to history and our existence. We are to orient our lives according to this fact, and discover significance by contributing to this overarching purpose. We are privileged to be part of something that will succeed and endure. Our labor is not in vain.

THE IMPORTANCE OF VOCATION

Our understanding of Christian spirituality finds its completion when we incorporate the element of self-denying participation in God's purposes in the world. The Christian life, as we have seen, is about connecting and it is about becoming. It is also, finally, about *doing*. Christ wants to live with us, dwell in us, and work *through* us. And this leads us to the matter of vocation.

It is interesting to listen to people today when they talk about their work. "What is your vocation?" someone may be asked. And not infrequently, especially if they are younger adults, they will answer: "Well, actually, I just have a job right now." There is a distinction in our minds between a vocation and a job. Being a doctor is a vocation. Working at Starbucks is usually a job. We all aspire toward vocations, and the status and salaries that go along with them. We endure jobs as necessities of life.

This way of thinking masks the true and historic meaning of vocation. The word comes from the Latin *vocare*, which means "to call." Historically, then, having a vocation meant that one had been called — *divinely* called and appointed, actually — to a particular line of work and way of life. We each have a calling upon our lives to participate in the purposes of God — to play a role in his grand designs to care for creation, to restore people to himself through Christ, and to build his kingdom.

God has revealed himself to be one who acts — who does things. He doesn't just sit around. Therefore to be in God's likeness also has a "doing" side for us. Imaging God involves a capacity for *creative* work, delegated sovereignty over the rest of creation, and participation in the redemptive and kingdom-building work which God is about in history. This is addressed and fulfilled in the vocational dynamic of Christian spirituality.

SOME BIBLICAL EXAMPLES

The Bible is full of stories of individuals who showed in their lives a healthy integration of all three dynamics of authentic spirituality. Moses met God at the burning bush, and was changed forever. The defeated fugitive became an empowered leader. He strode back into Egypt with a walking stick that could dangerously morph into a snake, and with a relentless demand of Pharaoh: "Let my people go!"

Isaiah had a dramatic vision of God in his magnificent holiness and glory (Isaiah 6). As the doorposts shook and the place filled with smoke, the prophet was overwhelmed with his own sinfulness, but was not allowed to wallow in it. A seraph placed a hot coal on Isaiah's tongue to signify his purification from sin. Isaiah would never be the same. Immediately he was invited to participate in the work God was doing in the world. "Who will go for us?" thundered the voice of God. And Isaiah responded in the rounding out of his spiritual experience, "Here am I. Send me!"

Jesus was baptized in the river Jordan by his cousin John. The relational dynamic is present as the Spirit descended as a dove from heaven and a voice said: "This is my Son, whom I love" (Matthew 3:17). Jesus was then led into the wilderness to strengthen his character by resisting temptation. But then he returned, full of the Holy Spirit, the gospel of Luke says, and launched his ministry — to preach the gospel, proclaiming freedom for prisoners and release for the oppressed.

The same thing happened with Saul on the road to Damascus, as we noted earlier. The pattern is consistent. Those who encounter God, and are changed by him, are never permitted to remain idle. The story cannot end with just relationship and transformation. God's Spirit inevitably stirs such people up to engage in useful service, to find their place in the grand scheme of God's higher purposes. "For we are God's handiwork, created in Christ Jesus to do good works, which God prepared in advance for us to do" (Ephesians 2:10).

THE GIFT OF COMMISSION

We came to Regent College in Vancouver in the late 1970s. The school had just taken a bold step of faith by hiring not one but two new theologians. One was J. I. Packer from England; the other was a German theologian by the name of Klaus Bockmuehl, who had studied under Karl Barth in Basel, Switzerland, and still spoke with a strong German accent. We discovered Bockmuehl's profound piety as we got to know him and were invited to his home. He walked with his God, invested in that relationship, and spoke of the inner life from personal experience. It was a great loss to us all when he died at midlife of a painful cancer. But one of the things he wrote before he died was a little book entitled *Living by the Gospel*.[3] The first half of the book describes the gifts we receive from the gospel, and the second half describes the duties that arise from the gospel. The structure made sense; we were used to thinking of the Christian life this way — what Christ gives us, and what we are obliged to return to him by way of duties and responsibilities. The first part is the good news, and the second part is the not-so-good stuff, so to speak.

But here was the amazing thing. Professor Bockmuehl put his chapter on our calling in the gift section. He called it the *gift* of commission! Why? Did he move the chapter over from its rightful place in the duties section just to give his table of contents more balance and a greater appearance of symmetry? Certainly not! No, he referred to our commission quite intentionally as a gift rather than a duty. He saw it, like the apostle Paul did, as an incredible blessing. He did so because our calling satisfies our deep need to be creatively useful, and gives us opportunity to invest our energies in something of significance. As Margaret Silf has said, "There is more to life than the mere management of our lives to achieve comfort and security."[4] Few gifts match the blessing of giving our lives to something that *matters*.

And where will we find this? We humans are cosmic amphibians. We stand astride the seen and the unseen. But we are creatures of the earth, fashioned from dust and destined to return to it. This is the sphere, full of suffering and conflict, in which we are called to do our work. Authentic Christian spirituality follows the pattern of the incarnation—it becomes flesh. Vocation is following the heart of God into the world.

THE PROBLEM OF MEANINGLESSNESS

Unlike our grandparents, only a few of us today learned the classic stories of Greek mythology in school. Nevertheless, most of us have a vague recollection of the myth of Sisyphus. According to Homer, this tragic figure had gotten on the bad side of the gods. As a result, the poor guy was blinded and doomed to push a massive rock up a mountain. With no choice but to try and fulfill his assignment, he strained and grunted, grinding his heels into the flinty ground for traction. But as soon as Sisyphus neared the peak, and the accomplishment of his task, the massive stone would roll back down to the bottom and he would have to start the arduous effort all over again. The cycle played out with numbing repetition and futility.

People have resonated with this story for thousands of years, finding in it something of their own life experience. Back in the 1940s, the existential philosopher Albert Camus dusted off the ancient myth of Sisyphus to make it a metaphor for the meaninglessness of modern life. I thought about this one day while visiting the Sorbonne campus of the University of Paris on the city's famed Left Bank. If you walk just a few blocks west along Rue St. Germain, you come to the Café Les Deux Magots, where Camus and compatriots Jean-Paul Sartre, Simone Bouvier, and others used to hang out together.

These thinkers had bleakly concluded that there was no meaning in life—no overarching direction or intent to human existence. This was painful to acknowledge, and they were well acquainted with the anger and even nausea this realization brought with it. Since there was no meaning to be *discovered* in life, their recommendation was that individuals should try to *create* their own. Camus suggested that if Sisyphus had only learned to accept the absurdity of his task, and resigned himself to it, he might possibly have been able to enjoy his ordeal.[5] For the last half century, this way of thinking has been spreading like an oil spill throughout popular culture.

It especially grieved me to notice that the Café Les Deux Magots is located right across a cobblestone lane from the front of the eleventh-century St. Germain des Pres on Paris's oldest continuing church site. Sartre and Camus huddled in the very shadow of the cross, pausing in their conversations until the church bells finished tolling, yet declining to embrace the purpose-filled Christian vision of life as their own.

It is very difficult to live life as these philosophers (and their postmodern successors) recommend—at least in a healthy and joyful way. The vocational dynamic of Christian spirituality addresses the problem of *meaninglessness* in life. Part of the anguish of life without God is from our inability to find meaning and purpose for our lives. The question of "Why?" dogs us ever more intensely as we age and see our end approaching. It explains our often unfulfilled longings for significance, our restless dilettantism, and our frenzied workaholism.

There is a simplistic kind of advice going around that we should content ourselves with just *being*, and not worry about *doing*. Such advice is meant to turn us back from a soul-atrophying activism, but it is wrongheaded nonetheless. We were designed to be doers too. The invitation to contribute to something that matters, to something bigger than our individual selves, is not a duty imposed, but an incredible gift. It is part of what makes our lives meaningful.

The Human Search for Meaning

Viktor Frankl was a Jewish survivor of the twentieth-century Holocaust—Adolf Hitler's malicious effort to exterminate the Jewish race. Frankl's reflections on his experience of concentration camps were published in a now-famous volume entitled *Man's Search for Meaning*. In this book, Frankl reflected on the variables that determined who managed to survive that awful ordeal and who did not. In most cases it came down to the intensity of the survivor's will to live. And the will to live, Frankl argued, depended on whether they were able to identify some meaning in their ongoing existence. "He who has a *why* to live for," he concluded in the words of Nietzsche, "can bear with almost any *how*."[6]

Most of us live lives that are cushioned from such a stark choice between life and death. But we are aware that burnout is a common phenomenon in our busy, competitive society. I recall my struggle a number of years ago with the early stages of it. I had given all I had, but my energy and enthusiasm had finally dried up. It was getting harder to sit up in the morning and swing my feet over the side of the bed. Then, on a book table at a pastor's conference my eyes fell upon a little book entitled *Clergy and Laity Burnout*. I grabbed it, took it back to my room, and read it straight through. One statement stood out above the rest. Burnout, the author explained, is seldom the result of an excessive workload. Rather, it is caused by the loss of a sense of meaning in what we are doing.[7] This was me; this was exactly my problem. A sense of meaning in our lives is what keeps us moving toward the future. We find sustained energy when we are engaged in something we believe really matters. Henry Scougal, a godly Scotsman of the last century, pointed out that every human being craves a cause worth exchanging their life for.

It's Not about Us

We see this theme in the life of Jesus himself. He and his disciples were traveling by foot from south to north, from Judea to Galilee, and of necessity passed through the in-between region of the alien Samaritans. There Jesus took a noon rest break beside the town's water supply while his disciples went to find food. While they were gone, Jesus started up a conversation with a Samaritan woman — an encounter that led to her life being transformed. By the time his followers came back with lunch, Jesus had lost interest in it. "My food," Jesus said, "is to do the will of him who sent me and to finish his work" (John 4:34).

Jesus' use of the word "food" is striking. It means that Jesus found his soul's nourishment, a healthy vitality and personal intensity, from the commission he had received from his heavenly Father. It was the same with the apostle Paul's sense of privilege in being called as an ambassador for Christ. We find real significance only as we are able to align ourselves with a goal greater than our own personal comfort and security. As my wise professor Bockmuehl put it, God's call upon our lives, his invitation to play a part in his unfolding plan for history, liberates us from drifting and from our natural egocentricity. "Feeding our ego occupies so much of our attention," he explained, "yet it is so notoriously too small an aim for a human being. [A person's] creational design is to serve a purpose bigger than his own sustenance."[8] God's call boosts us to a different plane of living.

Rick Warren states in the very first sentence of his book *The Purpose Driven® Life*, "It's not about you." That's just about the most countercultural thing anyone could say today. Yet this was undoubtedly part of what Jesus meant when he advised his followers in the Sermon on the Mount to "seek first [God's] kingdom and his righteousness, and all these things will be given to you as well" (Matthew 6:33). It *involves* us, but it is not primarily *about* us.

DIMENSIONS OF PURPOSE IN LIFE

Our ultimate purpose is to glorify God, and everything we do is meant to contribute to this goal (1 Corinthians 10:31). Each of us is unique, and we will end up doing different things. Nevertheless, we will all find our places in larger currents of divine purpose that carry us along. The will of God is like a mighty river, and we, like many small boats, are borne along in the direction of its flow. From Scripture we detect that this waterway consists of three great causes or tasks. Participating in them gives meaning and significance to our individual lives.

First, the creational mandate (Genesis 1 – 2) is our calling to steward the earth — caring for it while we responsibly manage its resources and explore its wonders. This is a mandate (or commission) that legitimizes the arts, science, medicine, industry, and the political sphere. Working in these areas is in no way inferior to "full-time Christian service" — an arbitrary mental construct if there ever was one!

Second, we are also called to participate in the redemptive work of God, by spreading the gospel (Matthew 28). God is constantly seeking "to draw people to himself for their own good,"[9] and we have been given a role in this. Jesus called his followers to proclaim an *embodied* gospel. As we noted in an earlier chapter, the church is to be more than merely a herald of the truth. The way it "does life" together, and shows compassion to the world, should make its testimony plausible and compelling. This is an integral part of fulfilling the evangelistic mandate.

Finally, there is the building of the kingdom (Matthew 6). Thousands of people live on top of Manila's mountainous garbage dump. The stench is sickening as they root through the smoldering refuse for the smallest salvage items; but this is their life. Mothers holding babies, and staring vacantly ahead, squat in the hot sun at the border between Tijuana and affluent San Diego. In their hands are little Styrofoam cups for donations from passersby. AIDS ravages African communities in which the chief cottage industry is the manufacture of rough coffins. A Christian family loses their teenage son to a drunk driver just weeks before his high school graduation, and they weep on the phone that they have lost their "little man of God." We hear the girl next door, who has a drug problem, crying out from her second-story bedroom balcony in the middle of the night. Infanticide is being justified in a botched partial-birth abortion when the baby accidentally slips out alive.

And so we pray, as Jesus taught us, for his kingdom to come, because it is the comprehensive solution to our myriad problems. Jesus inaugurated the "rule of God" in the world—a sphere in which blessing flows from acknowledging God's lordship in every aspect of living. We are called to *contribute* to the advance of this kingdom. Our individual callings in life will express God's unique plan for each one of us, and they will match who God has made us, and the abilities and inclinations we possess. But in one way or another, we will be fitting into these three great purposes of human existence. This is how we bring glory to God and where we find our true selves.

The biblical authors, and those who have imitated their faith, have always known that the challenge to live a godly life, to remain resilient in the face of opposition, and to be effective in advancing the kingdom, exceeds our natural human resources. Jesus reminded us, "Apart from me you can do nothing" (John 15:5). Paul, who understood Jesus' word of caution, also made a wonderful discovery on the positive side: "I can do all this through him who gives me strength" (Philippians 4:13).

The words of Hilary of Poitiers, from the fourth century, ring true today. In response to his own calling, he prayed: "If I am actually to do it, I must ask for your help and mercy, ask you to fill with wind the sails I have hoisted for you and to carry me forward on my course—to breathe, that is, your Spirit into my faith ... and to enable me to continue."[10] Like Hilary, we must become sailors, hoisting *our* sails so that the empowering wind, the very breath of God, can move us forward.

A HEART IN SYNC

I have a friend who was not a Christian when he began college. One of the student organizations at the school he attended in Chicago had organized Christmas hampers for needy families on the city's south side. The large boxes contained a turkey and other Christmas foods, along with candy and wrapped toys and gifts for the children. All the boxes had destinations, and had all been promised for delivery by Christmas Eve. My friend Paul had agreed to assist in the distribution.

One of the homes he was assigned on a very cold and snowy night was on the third floor of a cheap tenement house, accessible only by ascending three flights of rickety iron staircase on the outside of the building. Upon knocking, he was ushered into a small room in which a poor family of seven was squeezed together. The room was hot. Humidity clouded the window panes. The father was in his undershirt. But both parents were overwhelmed with gratitude. The children's eyes lit up with anticipation. There was a touching and memorable celebration of goodwill and hope. Self-conscious, Paul made his exit quickly.

To this day he believes that his Christian conversion occurred during his descent on the treacherous staircase. Something happened as he steadied himself against the shaking of the metal in the frigid winter wind. He felt something he had never experienced before. "For the first time in my life," he recalled many decades later, "I felt that my heart was beating in sync with the heart of God." He sensed intimacy with God and felt his approval. It felt so wonderful that he was drawn into the embrace of God from that moment on.

KNOWING GOD

It is one thing to know *about* God. It is another to know God in the sense of personal encounter with him. So much of the literature of Christian spirituality is designed to move us from mere information about God to experiential connection with him. Yet knowing God in the *fullest* sense goes beyond even relational intimacy.

If you know someone well, you have a pretty good idea how they are wired and what makes them tick. In other words, you know their disposition. And if you know someone's disposition, you can predict pretty accurately how they will respond to specific events, crises, and people in the future. You are able to anticipate how they will react, because you have already measured the set of their sails.

God has a predictable character too. We may call it the divine disposition. He is naturally predisposed to act in certain ways. He hates injustice, for example, and intervenes on behalf of people who are oppressed. He is slow to get angry and has an extravagant capacity for love (Psalm 103:8). These qualities, and others revealed in Scripture, make up the divine disposition — God's signature way of being and responding to events on planet earth.

According to Scripture, knowing God is supposed to include *participating* in the divine disposition. Knowing God in the fullest sense means that we adopt his disposition as our own. Our character, values, and conduct are to line up with his (Jeremiah 22:16; Philippians 3:10). This may seem to us like a strangely inflated definition, but knowing him in the fullest sense really is this holistic. It includes living according to the impulses of God's own heart. One of the most powerful forms of union is the unity of common purpose, and this is exactly what we can experience with God when our disposition resonates with his.[11]

Jesus once said, "I am the good shepherd; I know my sheep and my sheep know me — just as the Father knows me and I know the Father — and I lay down my life for the sheep" (John 10:14–15). It is common to assume that this passage contains two unrelated facts: (1) that Jesus knew the Father, and (2) that he had decided to sacrifice his life on the cross. Actually, these two things are closely connected. Jesus understands that the Father's disposition is sacrificial love, and he *knows* the Father in the sense that he is going to live out that same spirit himself. There is an obvious invitation here to the "sheep" as well — since they *know* Christ, they should also be prepared to surrender to the same disposition — which is, supremely, a disposition of sacrificial love.

How does this work out in practice? In the next chapter, we will focus on ways to discern God's personal calling on our lives, and how we can keep in step with the guiding voice of his Spirit in a lifelong journey with him.

————————— ✑ SOME HELPFUL GUIDES ✑ —————————

AUGUSTINE OF HIPPO (354 – 430 AD)

Augustine was one of the church's most significant theologians and a profound contributor to its spirituality. We have highlighted how his vision of the *City of God* (426 AD) sustained Christian hope and purpose during a collapse of empire, but his volume entitled *Confessions* has been at least as influential. This latter classic was pioneering in the psychological depth of its candid self-reflections; its most quoted prayer is: "You have made us for yourself, and our hearts are restless until they find rest in you."

JOHN BUNYAN (1628 – 1688)

Bunyan was an English Puritan spiritual writer, jailed more than once for his church principles. He wrote a number of books of enduring influence in the English-speaking world, including *Grace Abounding to the Chief of Sinners* and especially *Pilgrim's Progress* (1684). This latter work, probably the most celebrated example of the journey motif in Christian spiritual writing, underscores the truth that the Christian life, though difficult, is goal oriented, purposeful, and worthwhile.

RICK WARREN

Rick Warren pastors Saddleback Church in Orange County, California, one of the largest Protestant churches in America. Warren's two bestsellers, *The Purpose Driven® Church* and *The Purpose Driven® Life*, have touched a deep need in America and worldwide. Warren himself has become active in ministry to desperate people in Africa—living out his fifth thesis, namely, that we discover purpose in living through service to others.

CHAPTER SUMMARY

The Christian life involves connecting, becoming, and *doing*. In this chapter we began our study of the vocational dynamic of Christian spirituality—God's gracious solution to the apparent futility of human existence. It is an incredible gift to be called to purposeful living and to contribute to a cause greater than ourselves. We discover meaning in life by aligning ourselves with God's invitation to steward the creation, evangelize the nations, and build his kingdom. A spiritual life, as Evelyn Underhill has explained, is one that is self-given to the greater movement of God's will. Knowing God in the fullest sense requires a heart that beats in sync with his own and a willingness to follow it into the world.

THE GIFT OF
A PERSONAL CALLING

I will instruct you and teach you in the way you should go;
I will counsel you with my loving eye on you.
Psalm 32:8

The Chateau Frontenac stands high atop the old town of Quebec City. The stately landmark offers a panoramic view of the fertile St. Lawrence River valley, where the first French settlers arrived in the early 1600s. Sheltered upstream behind this fortress grew La Nouvelle-France, a tiny colony strung out along the shores of the great waterway, with its back hard up against virgin forests. I stood beneath the Chateau one day with my French-speaking daughter Claire, gazing down at the fortifications and bulky cannons that once guarded the colony—now a vista of quaintly painted shops, jazz players, cobblestone lanes, and huge Great Lakes freighters sliding along in the distant haze.

I recalled how this French colony had been founded partly as a base for the evangelization of the natives and the beginning of a godly society—a Christian civilization—that would eventually extend throughout the interior regions of the North American continent. This inspiring project attracted some of the best and most zealous Christians in France—men and women alike—and prominent among them the remarkable Marie of the Incarnation (1599–1672).

Marie was born in the French city of Tours, and got her nickname from her many visions of Christ. She lived during a revival of Christian mysticism—a renewal movement characterized by dreams, ecstatic experiences, and radical devotion. From childhood Marie fully embraced this exciting new religious atmosphere. She was just nineteen when her husband died, leaving her with an infant son and a nearly bankrupt family business. She resisted the social pressure to remarry, and during a retreat in 1620 had the first of a series of mystical experiences that shaped her devotion and determined her vocation. Her strong sense of a special vocation persisted for years thereafter, despite the need to defer her calling in order to stabilize the business she had inherited.[1]

Finally, a decade later, she made arrangement for the care of her twelve-year-old son, Claude, and then entered a cloister. It tore her maternal heart to leave her child, but her resolve was intense. Stimulated by the latest reports from pioneer Jesuit missionaries in New France (now the Canadian province of Quebec), and powerful visions of herself in future missionary service in a wilderness setting—visions that came to include explicit reference to Canada—she concluded that she had been called to evangelistic ministry in the New World.

Before long she received approval from her superiors, and with that a one-way ticket to North America. She survived a hazardous three-month crossing of the Atlantic and arrived in Quebec in 1639. The beleaguered French outpost contained barely three hundred persons at the time, was isolated to the extreme, and the winters were unbelievably harsh. But Marie never looked back; for the next thirty-three years she played a prominent role in the emerging society of French Canada.

She devoted herself to educating French and Indian girls, and established the first school for girls in North America. She wrote extensively on theology and spirituality, carried on a lively correspondence, and engaged in translation projects for the indigenous Iroquois and Algonquin tribes. Her mysticism never impaired her shrewd business and political instincts. She remained prominent in civil affairs throughout. She belongs to an elite group of powerful women who made pioneering contributions to French society and culture in North America. She was a lioness.

She and her son, Claude, who became a monk, stayed in contact through letters across the years. Her ambivalent feelings about leaving him seem apparent in comments like this, which she once made to him: "You have been abandoned by your mother ... yet hasn't this abandonment been to your advantage? I had to obey his divine will." Equally telling was Claude's response, which was to wish his mother every success in her desire to become a martyr![2]

Marie of the Incarnation's life stands out in contrast to the relatively obscure lives of most of her female contemporaries. Throughout her colorful career she never questioned her vocation. Should we? Is there reason to be skeptical of her claim to a missionary calling mediated through an unusual series of visions? Was she simply a well-intentioned, but nonetheless misguided person? If so, how should we account for the remarkable authority and lasting impact of her life? Her story is just one of many that highlight the question of how we should discern our vocation.

Framing the Issue

God invites us to reconnect with him (and others), be renewed in Christ, and find fulfillment by contributing to his purposes. What we do, and how we invest the fleeting years of our lives, is enormously important. Yet it is not merely a consequence of our spirituality. It is an intrinsic element of it. Authentic Christian spirituality is about more than prayer and contemplation. It is about living all of life before God, and this means that what we *do* is significant. We have each been called to live purposefully. There are customized places and roles for each of us within the generous boundaries of God's overarching mandates to steward creation, proclaim the gospel, and advance his kingdom on earth.

Still, a basic question remains. How do we discern our personal calling in life? How do we know where we fit in the grand scheme of things? In response to our anxiety God offers this promise: "I will instruct you and teach you in the way you should go; I will counsel you with my loving eye on you" (Psalm 32:8). So we need not worry whether he will direct us, or whether his intentions for us are rooted in love. At the same time we should not be passive. Good religion does not arrest human development. We are to grow up into adults who reflect on Scripture and experience, investigate options rigorously, and practice wisdom in our vocational decision making.

Naturally we would like the finalized script up front. That would reduce our anxiety and give us a greater feeling of control. But the light God provides for our path usually illuminates only a few steps ahead. The story lines of our lives cannot be predicted with complete accuracy, nor the precise contours of our callings fully anticipated. From time to time we may catch a glimpse—a sneak peek before the curtain goes up—of God's design for our lives. But living out a vocation requires an ongoing relationship with God. We do not so much discover God's will in a "total package" sense as we align ourselves, at this moment, with God.[3]

In times past most people locked into careers early, with precious little opportunity to change things around later on. But life in affluent modern societies is more fluid. Careers have trajectories, and these often take twists and turns. Nevertheless, the segments of the working lives of happy people will not be totally eclectic. Most likely there will be a consistent orientation to our lives—a certain kind of work and ministry toward which we naturally gravitate, and in which we find special satisfaction.

The Freedom of Being a Team Member

My friend Ray had a winsome spirit and a remarkable gift of evangelism. I wanted so much to be a successful evangelist like him. I fell asleep some nights working up apologetic answers to every conceivable objection to faith. I even paid to attend a nationally recognized evangelism training program. Then, after taking a deep breath, I tackled the door-to-door strategy. When Ray went to a door on a cold call, people would welcome him in as the messenger they had been praying would come. When I knocked, they were more likely to tell me to get lost and threaten to call the cops.

It didn't seem fair at first. But after some struggle I realized that God's work in the world has been assigned to the *whole* church. We are each to contribute to it, but always in a way that is consistent with the gifts we have. The entire burden of building the kingdom was never meant to rest on any single pair of shoulders. Finally I could celebrate Ray's gift, and get on with *my* own assigned task and calling.

Another experience marked a turning point in my life. I was in my midtwenties and painfully certain that the marketing position I had with IBM was not my true calling in life. So eventually I just flat out quit. Maybe it wasn't the smartest move from a cash-flow perspective, but it was a huge relief. For about six months after that, I kept myself alive on odd jobs and my parents' hospitality. I needed to figure out what to do with my life. I had always done well academically. As a kid I actually looked forward to going back to school every fall. I loved the refurbished gloss on the squeaky hardwood gym floor, the smell of Elmer's glue, and the grind of the pencil sharpener at the back of the room. A new binder of lined paper was a fresh invitation to attempt perfection.

My perspective on vocation was seriously skewed by the fact that I grew up in a religious environment that was suspicious of the intellectual life. We took William Carey over John Calvin hands down, and a soul winner over a theologian every time. Our preachers never failed to get a laugh when they deliberately confused the words "seminary" and "cemetery." In a seriously abridged rendition of 1 Corinthians 8:1, we were led to believe that *knowledge* "puffeth up" (King James Version). Whatever that meant, it didn't sound good.

The Ontario Museum of Art is devoted to outstanding homegrown Canadian artistry. I sat on a bench there one day about this time, surrounded by the best of the best. In front, as I recall it now, were works by Tom Thomson and the Group of Seven, with their surreal depictions of bleak pines and gnarly swamps on the rock-faced Canadian Shield that encircles Hudson's Bay. To my left was a huge Emily Carr canvas of dark greens and grotesque totem faces, inspired by the Pacific rain forests of the Queen Charlotte Islands. Even a novice can recognize the distinctive talents of Thomson, Carr, or A. Y. Jackson.

These artists had work hanging in this prestigious gallery for one reason only: they were very good at what they did. But then it hit me—none of them painted the same way. They used different materials, selected different subjects, and created different moods. Their brush strokes, their choices of color, the way each one went about their craft, was *uniquely* their own. If they had conformed to a template, the result would have been mediocre. Instead, each filtered truth and beauty through their distinct personality and talent. That was their genius and my permission. I walked back to the subway with a spring in my step for the first time in months.

None of us is called to do everything. The work of God has been assigned to the whole people of God. We are simply called to do our part. God's purposes are best achieved when the different contributors stay focused on their assigned roles. We should not pursue a particular role in life because, according to our calculation, it will bring strategic influence with it. Such calculations tend to be driven mainly by ego and ambition. Among the options that are realistically available to us, we have God's permission to aspire to roles than seem to reflect who we really are. This truth can be a tremendous source of freedom.

Joy *and* Usefulness

Some Christians think that God's will is always *contrary* to our own, and can actually be identified by this signature: If something is of God, they reason, you're not going to like it. Such thinking is based on a serious misrepresentation of God's true heart. The fact is that our happiness is important to God, and his calling on our lives will always be in accord with our deepest identity.

One of the most insightful—certainly most frequently quoted—
comments on Christian vocation is by Frederick Buechner: "The place
God calls you to is the place where your deep gladness and the world's
deep hunger meet."[4] God generally calls us to what we need to do and
what the world needs to have done. In order to discover our personal
calling, then, we must be acquainted with God's heart for the world,
and in touch with who we are. Vocation emerges where these two deep
realities make contact.

Both parts of the equation are musts. Suppose someone gets a kick
out of shooting beer commercials for television. This may seem to be
working well for them, but they are still wide of the mark on what
the world needs to have done. On the other hand, a medical doctor in
a leper colony in the Third World is definitely doing something that
the world needs done. But suppose they hate the work, dread getting
up each day, and are becoming more depressed all the time. They feel
like a square peg in a round hole. Clearly they have still not discovered
what they need to be doing.[5]

A Christian's personal vocation, therefore, will consist of passionate, motivated engagement in something of useful service to the
world.[6] If we agree with Irenaeus that the glory of God is a person
fully alive, then this formula is also key to glorifying God. Invari-
ably God's call involves service. Yet because the specific form of our
service will be tailored to our inclinations and aptitudes, it will tend
to be energizing rather than draining—even if it also happens to be
difficult at times.

Buechner's insight into the elements of a personal calling might
profit from a slight tweaking. For the sake of greater precision, let's
substitute *passion* for gladness,[7] and *need* for hunger. Our revised statement now proposes that our calling lies where our personal passion—
the thing that deeply moves and energizes us—intersects with the
world's compelling need. The term "passion" may better express what
unique individuals bring to the equation. Using "gladness" risks leaving the impression that discipleship is always upbeat and cheerful,
when in fact it can be costly, difficult, and tearful. It tends, after all, to

replicate the pattern of suffering-death-resurrection experienced first by Jesus.

As a Christian, the Danish philosopher Søren Kierkegaard was shocked by God's demand, recorded in Genesis, that Abraham offer his son Isaac as a human sacrifice.[8] Abraham ended up not having to follow through on the execution, but Kierkegaard never got over his sense that God's call, then and now, can seem unreasonable and even outrageous to our way of thinking. Responding well to God's call, though it is key to our fulfillment, can still be difficult. It requires us to swim upstream—in some cases, to be fools for Christ. God's calling will be a good fit for our gifts and abilities, and especially for our passion. But it will just as surely move us beyond our comfort zone.

OPTIMAL CONDITIONS FOR DISCERNMENT

A person with talent who wants to honor God still needs something else—and that something is discernment. Discernment is the ability to sort out with an eagle eye what's really going on, and then choose wisely and well from among the alternatives on the table. This is a necessary competency, for unfortunately other voices—a powerful media with skewed values, our own creative subconscious, and the whispers of the Deceiver—compete with the voice of God in our lives. How are we to know the truth?

The optimal conditions for discerning God's call upon our lives begin with a willingness to listen. According to a familiar Bible story, the boy Samuel was awakened one night by a persistent voice (1 Samuel 3). The experience was so disconcerting that he ran to sleeping Eli, his old mentor, for advice. Eli instructed him to respond the next time it happened with: "Speak, LORD, for your servant is listening" (v. 9). It was classic advice—applicable to Samuel and all those who have sought guidance ever since. Attentiveness does not come naturally to us, but listening prayer is integral to discerning vocation.

Jesus mentioned another condition when he said: "Blessed are the pure in heart, for they will see God" (Matthew 5:8). In Scripture the heart is the affective center of our beings—the core of who we are. But why did Jesus insist on *purity* there? Because, as he explains later on (6:22), our heart functions like our eye—as a chief means of insight. It must be pure in order to function reliably. Unresolved conflicts and denials—what Ignatius of Loyola called "disordered affections"—will cloud our spiritual lenses so that we will be unable to discern truthfully. God cannot reveal things to us if we are a tangle of self-deceptions and rationalizations.[9] We will become, in the words of Scripture, darkened in our understanding (Romans 1:21; Ephesians 4:18).

The saints have always known this. One of the great words of wisdom in Proverbs is that "the integrity of the upright guides them, but the unfaithful are destroyed by their duplicity" (11:3). We have to *want* the truth, and *love* the truth, before we will ever be able to *know* the truth.[10] Purity of heart gets us in touch with our true selves. This is a huge advantage, for God seldom writes in the clouds or thunders in a deep bass voice that echoes for miles. He speaks through our own unvoiced thoughts. As Dallas Willard has insightfully observed, "All of the guidance which we are going to receive from God, no matter what the external or internal accompaniments may be, will ultimately take the form of our own thoughts and perceptions."[11]

It is not God's characteristic style to reveal too much of our true vocation until we have settled whether we will obey his call. He does not submit a detailed proposal for our perusal, in the hope that we might possibly accept the terms of his offer. The call of God requires consecration up front. Abraham, the father of our faith, is our example on this. "By faith Abraham, when called to go to a place he would later receive as his inheritance, obeyed and went, even though he did not know where he was going" (Hebrews 11:8).

Francis de Sales, whom we have already met, was a champion of what he called the devout life. His definition of Christian devotion is instructive. It is, he suggested, a life of *ready* obedience rooted in love for God. Genuinely Christian devotion, he insisted, is never reluctant, grudging, or conditional, but always characterized by an enthusiastic, eager, and cheerful eagerness to obey.[12]

The Familiar Speaking Voice

Once these optimal conditions exist, we can move on to the question of how to recognize God calling us to a particular vocation.[13] Many helpful resources, and a wealth of advice, are available today, so I will mention just one factor—the element of familiarity—and illustrate it with a personal anecdote. Russ and I were close friends in high school. We played on the basketball and football teams, and hung out together after school and on weekends. After graduation, however, things changed. We both moved away. Russ went off to find himself in Australia, and I ended up in another part of the country. As we drifted apart geographically, eventually we lost contact.

Years passed—about twenty-five in all. During that long spell my friend became a successful lawyer and I became a Bible college professor. Along the way we each got married and started families. And then, coincidentally, our family moved to the very city in which my old friend was practicing law. He had a thriving practice and was highly regarded in the community. I felt inferior by comparison, and hesitated to try to reconnect with him. One day—I'm not sure what made me do it—I finally phoned his office. Without identifying myself I asked the receptionist to put my call through directly to him. When he answered, I said, "Well, Russ, how are you?"

"Wait!" he said. "Don't tell me. Wait …." My voice must have sounded vaguely familiar to him. I could sense that he was trying to scan back through long-neglected sectors of his memory for a match. "Wait," he said once more, buying a couple of extra seconds. And then in triumph he shouted out my surname. "It's you!" he said. I was relieved and totally delighted that he still remembered the sound of my voice. It was a lasting result of our boyhood friendship. But that's the way it is with family and close friends. We hear the voice, and we can just tell.

Jesus made a similar point in response to the Pharisees' hostility toward him. When it is time for sheep to head out to pasture, he explained, the shepherd leads them out, "and his sheep follow him because they know his voice" (John 10:4). The Pharisees failed to pick up on it. He sounded like an imposter to them. It was all about voice recognition—something that comes with familiarity.

THE ORDINARY BECOMES TINGED WITH GLORY

In chapter 12 of Romans, the apostle Paul urges believers to offer themselves to God as living sacrifices, and then to be transformed by the renewing of their minds. Then they will experience the will of God for themselves, and discover that it is good and pleasing and perfect (vv. 1–2). Usually we stop here, but the passage actually continues: "Do not think of yourself more highly than you ought, but rather think of yourself with sober judgment, in accordance with the faith God has distributed to each of you" (v. 3). If we are to discover God's will, we will also need, in addition to consecration and cognitive restructuring, some sober self-realization.

Paul understood the problem of vanity—our tendency to judge ourselves more talented than we really are. What does this have to do with aligning ourselves with the will of God? Quite a bit, actually! You see, the roots of our self-deception lie in our deep-seated and anxious sense of inadequacy.[14] We sense how high the expectations are, and we pretend—deliberately deceiving ourselves—that we are sufficient to meet them. So we drive ourselves, yet despite our workaholic effort we remain perpetually dissatisfied. In reality we are running scared. It is terrifying to look honestly in the mirror—to "think of [ourselves] with sober judgment."

A friend of mine is a gifted theologian who writes faster and is more sought after than I am. He was invited to speak at a session of the prestigious American Academy of Religion, and I decided to attend in support. As his presentation began, I whispered to a colleague next to me: "The speaker up there is a personal friend of mine." But from the very beginning, I found my friend's remarks and attitude strangely irritating. As usual, he was brilliant, but I began making sarcastic asides under my breath, offering a series of unsolicited and petty criticisms. Some things I said were downright mean-spirited. Finally, my colleague sitting next to me turned and looked me right in the eye. "Did you say that the speaker was your *friend*?"

His words hit me like a crowbar across the forehead. My envy was exposed, and the conviction overwhelming. The moment the speech was over I stood up and headed straight back to my hotel room. I knelt down beside my bed and wept out my confession to God. Underlying my jealously was fear that my relative ordinariness left me without value and might easily disqualify me from a truly useful role in God's service.

The way out of this darkness was first to recall in a deep way that God's unconditional love embraces me despite my being unspectacular. The other thing, as the apostle Paul indicated, is that God's perfect will is always discovered within the boundaries of our *actual* abilities and limitations. It is never discovered through frantically overreaching ourselves. The poet W. H. Auden put it well when he said: "Even the most commonplace things are tinged with glory."[15]

We can use the gifts we have, and accept their relative size— which is what "in accordance with the faith God has distributed to each" seems to mean. It's liberating when we realize that we can put our energy into the fulfilling use of *our gifts*, such as they are, and enjoy the experience of being creative and making genuine contributions to the cause of Christ. Serenity comes by accepting our identity and engaging in diligent service. Instead of trying to be something or someone we're not, we can give our attention with joy to the task of being all *we* were meant to be.

HOPE AND COURAGE

I still don't know quite what to make of Marie of the Incarnation's decision to leave her son for a stellar missionary career in New France. But I do know that most of us can look back on our lives and recall decisions we would like to have back. We came to a certain fork in the road, and now, in hindsight, it seems that maybe we went the wrong way. And if so, the question that haunts us is this: If we fell off the wagon of God's best plan back then, is there any hope of climbing back on?

Indeed there is, and perhaps I can illustrate it this way. If you are on a well-designed website, no matter how complex it may be, you will never be more than a click away from the "home page" and an opportunity to start over. That's because return loops were coded into the software to allow you this option. It seems to me that this is how God guides our lives after we have strayed from his vocational design for us. Our heavenly Father is the great salvage operator who is always able to craft from the chaos of our messed-up lives a remarkably meaningful future. In *all things* he works for the good of those who love him (Romans 8:28). Grace is about second—and third and fourth—chances, and God is the creator *par excellence* of new beginnings.

Our focus has been on discerning our personal vocation in life. But *knowing* what we have been called to do is no guarantee that we will follow through and actually *do* it. Jesus concluded his Sermon on the Mount with a story about two house builders—a foolish one who built on sand and a wise one who built on a rock foundation. Likewise, Jesus explained, wise people are those who hear his words and *put them into practice* (Matthew 7:24). This follow-up step is crucial.

We may balk at obedience because the prospect seems disagreeable to us, or it may appear too daunting. At a certain point we switch from needing information to requiring courage.[16] Even before Christ, the Greeks recognized that courage belongs among the most important human virtues. It is the strength to face down our fears for the sake of a higher, more compelling obligation. Joshua needed it (Joshua 1:9), Paul prayed for it (Ephesians 6:19–20), and Jesus modeled it in the events leading to his execution.

Throughout Asia the lion—often called the *singh*—has long been revered as a symbol of courage and valor. There is, for example, a statue of a lion in the harbor of Singapore—which, as its name suggests, is Lion City. Regardless of where on earth we live, we will experience joy and meaning by embracing God's unique call and claim on our lives. When we do so, we also become eligible for an infusion of the Lion of Judah's own Spirit. That, more than anything else, ensures that our calling will not be a burden but an incredible gift.

We have now concluded our study of the three dynamics of Christian spirituality.

Next we will examine how we should live in light of all this. We will review the importance of an integrated spirituality, and then consider how to move forward with disciplined intent.

∽ SOME HELPFUL GUIDES ∽

IGNATIUS OF LOYOLA (1491 – 1556)

Loyola was a Basque soldier who converted into a soldier of Jesus Christ. A passion for Christian service, including missionary work, pervades his thought. He founded the Jesuits, an order known for its high standards, complete consecration to Christ, and rigorous attention to personal spiritual discipline. *The Spiritual Exercises*, a formation manual Loyola wrote, continues to be a valued guide to the spiritual life for many who live their vocations beyond the boundaries of the order he founded.

PARKER PALMER

Palmer has been nourished in the Quaker tradition of Christianity, one noted for its contemplative side and, at times, its active commitment to causes of social justice. Quakers, for example, helped to establish colonial Pennsylvania as a haven of religious tolerance. In *The Active Life*, Palmer emphasizes the importance of a spirituality that engages the world in life-giving action. In *Let Your Life Speak*, he shows how the inner voice of our true selves holds the key to discovering our God-given vocation.

GORDON SMITH

Gordon Smith is a contemporary evangelical with years of missionary service and an ecumenical vision of Christian spirituality. He is well acquainted with the spiritualities of Ignatius of Loyola and John Wesley, has a special interest in spiritual discernment and vocational calling, and appreciates the communal as well as the personal aspects of each. Among his writings on these topics are *Listening to God in Times of Choice, Courage and Calling*, and *The Voice of Jesus*.

Chapter Summary

What we *do* with our lives is an essential element of true spirituality. Within the locus of God's overarching purposes is a unique personal calling—a vocation—for each of us. The work and place to which God calls us will always be located at the intersection of our deep passion and the world's great need, for personal fulfillment and useful service are inextricably bound together. We must not be terrified by our ordinariness either, for God has creative ways of infusing it with significance. Likewise our past failures never disqualify us from the hope of a significant life. But we do require two things: knowledge of our calling and the Spirit-empowered courage to follow it.

An Integrated
Spirituality

*As Jesus grew up, he increased in wisdom
and in favor with God and people.*

Luke 2:52

H e was a free-spirited, drug-using California hippie in the 1960s
when he found God in an arid mountain canyon above Palm
Springs. Immediately Lonnie Frisbee felt called to be an evangelist.
His long hair and unkempt beard bore an unmistakable resemblance
to a now-famous (but speculative, of course) artist's depiction of Jesus
knocking at a closed cottage door. Lonnie cheerfully explained the
similarity by saying that there was no one he'd rather look like. He
became the quintessential Jesus freak—the poster boy of the Jesus
People movement.

The counterculture was in full swing up and down the West Coast
when Lonnie showed up barefoot on the doorstep of Chuck Smith,
founder of the Calvary Chapels. Smith and his wife were drawn to
the young man, and before long Lonnie assumed a prominent position in the movement. His success as an evangelist was remarkable,
and his gifts of supernatural healing were astonishing. Critics dis-
missed him as a charlatan, but most people acknowledged that he
had an unusual spiritual anointing. Thousands flocked to him. In

the early 1970s, pictures of him preaching and baptizing crowds of joyous young converts in the Pacific Ocean made the pages of *Time* and *Life* magazines.

After some time he drifted out of the Calvary Chapel orbit and into the emerging Vineyard network of John Wimber. There his charismatic ministry had a comparable impact, and helped to shape and confirm the distinctive "signs and wonders" emphasis of the Vineyard. He and Wimber took their power evangelism ministry around the world. In retrospect, "two of the largest evangelical denominations to emerge in the last thirty years bear his spiritual imprint."[1]

There were some signs throughout this period that all was not well in Lonnie's private life. His marriage had dissolved some years before. He carried some unhealed wounds from traumatic experiences during his childhood. There were occasional rumors of suspicious behavior or impropriety, but most people close to him considered the power of his ministry as proof that the rumors were unfounded or at least exaggerated.

Then the shocking news broke that Lonnie had AIDS, and out tumbled the secret that he had been in homosexual relationships for many years. The Calvary Chapel and Vineyard movements were devastated. Few people knew how to respond appropriately. He was abruptly removed from office. A curtain of shamed silence fell down around him. Lonnie died in 1993, still young and estranged from most of the people he had worked with and helped lead to faith.

A while ago I attended a Los Angeles viewing of a documentary on Lonnie's life.[2] Afterward, the director came on stage and fielded questions from the audience. It was moving to see middle-aged people (some of them conspicuously tattooed) get up in the dimly lit theater and say, "Lonnie led me to the Lord," or "Lonnie discipled me for three years; it's because of him that I'm in the ministry today." Many emotions surfaced during that time of collective reflection, but the element of tragedy in Lonnie Frisbee's life was unmistakable. The vocational dynamic of his life was powerful, but the transformational dynamic had been relatively underdeveloped. Perhaps the Christian community was at least partly responsible for this state of affairs. In any event, it is a sad reminder that the dynamics of Christian spirituality may be able to function independently of one another for a while, but long-term spiritual health certainly requires that all three be nurtured and sustained.

THE THREE-DIMENSIONAL CALL OF JESUS

People in first-century Palestine were intrigued with the possibility that a carpenter from Nazareth might be the Messiah who would finally deliver them from their enemies. The free bread, which he seemed able effortlessly to create, was also extremely appealing. They did not want to let him out of their sight. But Jesus indicated in pointed terms what would be required of those who chose to throw in their lot with him. "Whoever wants to be my disciple must deny themselves and take up their cross daily and follow me" (Luke 9:23).

Those who wish to live in close relationship to Jesus—those who apply, in other words, to become his disciples—must be prepared for at least two things. They must relinquish the self-absorption and personal ambition that have been the driving forces of their lives to this point. They must *deny* themselves. And they would not be allowed to indulge in the luxury of a detached and private friendship with Christ. They must get ready to obediently *follow* him out into a risky world of witness and service.

This is still the call of Christ to those who would be Christians. And the important thing to note is that this is not three calls bundled together, from which we are at liberty to select the one or two that we like, and leave the rest alone. It is a single call Christ gives, and the elements of it cannot be separated from one another. The Christian life is about living in relation to God, being transformed by the impulses of his divine life, and actively participating in God's purposes in the world.

The work of the Holy Spirit is central to Christian spirituality, and the Spirit, like Jesus, actively encourages all three dimensions. He encourages the relational dynamic through his assuring and uniting work. He actively assures us that the relationship we are counting on is real, and we do belong to God. He testifies to our spirits that we *are* the children of God (Romans 8:15–16). He also nurtures unity—arresting the alienating impulses of sin, prompting grace and forgiveness, and restoring harmony and *shalom* to human relationships. It is by the Spirit that we were all baptized so as to form one body (1 Corinthians 12:13). Little wonder, then, that the Scriptures urge us to "make every effort to keep *the unity of the Spirit* through the bond of peace" (Ephesians 4:3).

Likewise the Spirit promotes the transformational impulse of Christian spirituality. He does so by his works of moral refining and soul-healing. The Spirit's work of moral renewal is beautifully described in Galatians 5, where the fruit of the Spirit stand in striking contrast to the acts of the sinful flesh. After agonizing struggles with his own sinful nature, Paul finally discovered that the Spirit had set him free from the law of sin and death (Romans 8:2). Both Peter and Paul refer to the sanctifying work of the Spirit (1 Peter 1:2; 2 Thessalonians 2:13). With respect to healing, the anointing oil used in the healing ordinances of the church (James 5:14) is also a symbol of the Holy Spirit.

Finally, the Spirit contributes to the vocational dynamic by guiding and empowering believers. His ministry of guidance is apparent throughout the book of Acts, from the story of how he led Philip to appear alongside the Ethiopian eunuch's chariot, to Paul's decision, following the Macedonian call in a vision, to venture beyond Asia to bring the gospel into Europe for the first time. When the Spirit came at Pentecost, the disciples acquired power for effective service that Jesus had promised to them (Acts 1:8). The subsequent ministries of the early church were conducted in the power of the Spirit. Where the Holy Spirit is a manifest presence in lives, these three elements—the relational, the transformational, and the vocational—all seem to be naturally present as well. And the appropriate response on our part, as Paul explains, is to "keep in step with the Spirit" (Galatians 5:25).

An Interconnected Web

These three dynamics are vitally connected to one another. Logically, of course, everything begins with our relationship to God and the improved quality of other relationships that can develop out of this. Experiencing grace and feeling acceptance is the heart of it. "Nothing," says Gordon Smith, "is so fundamental to the Christian journey as knowing and feeling that we are loved. Nothing."[3] Our new sense of self—our new identity—is grounded in the amazing value God places on us.

But then, in the intimacy of such a personal relationship to him, something of God's own character gradually spills over into ours as a matter of contagious holiness and reflected glory. It stimulates our transformation. And from our awareness of his acceptance of us comes an increased confidence and boldness to face life's challenges and opportunities. The experience of being loved unconditionally has a profound effect on us—motivating and empowering us to take more risks. It becomes the platform for a whole new approach of courageous living.

Being familiar with God's disposition helps us anticipate how he would have us respond to new situations that come up in our lives. According to Jesus' metaphor, the sheep can recognize the voice of their Shepherd (John 10:4). Our lives then become less about doing things for God, and more about God doing his will through us. We must not forget that God is the source of our new life and spiritual power. Without sustained encounter with him, Christianity deteriorates into a humanly manufactured and humanly sustained enterprise. We end up only charging around, on the verge of exhaustion, desperately trying to keep things from collapsing.

But the transformational and vocational impulses also rebound to deepen and enrich our connection to God in Christ. A sanctified heart is more in tune with the Spirit of God than one cluttered and desensitized by besetting sin. The psalmist knew that if he willfully nursed iniquity in his heart, the Lord would not listen to him (Psalm

66:18). One of the central convictions of historic monasticism has been that soul-purification is a prerequisite to drawing close to God. This insight can, and has been, distorted into a burdensome legalism. But as long as it is understood within a framework of grace, it remains a worthy insight.

Similarly, our relationship with God is enriched by obediently living out our vocation in the world. Who did Jesus consider his mother and brothers—his real family? The ones who could expect to enjoy the closest relationship with Jesus were not his blood relatives, but those who were prepared to do the will of his Father in heaven (Matthew 12:50). On another occasion Jesus explained to his disciples, "Anyone who loves me will obey my teaching. My Father will love them, and we will come to them and make our home with them" (John 14:23). The spiritual flow starts with a love for God that expresses itself in obedient action and lifestyle. God's response is to draw even closer, settle in, make his home with them, and establish his presence more fully. Everything comes full circle. It starts in loving relationship and ends in even deeper connection.

There are many other examples of the interconnectedness of the spiritual dynamics. Jesus observed that if you make a tree good, its fruit will be good (Matthew 12:33). Who we are, in other words, will determine what we do. And once again there is a flip side. Our choices and behaviors also shape who we are becoming. As William May has observed, "We function not simply as agents producing deeds, but partly as authors and co-authors of our very beings."[4] We could go on, but I trust that by now the point is clear. The three dynamics are interwoven. Each fuels and feeds off the other two, and each is essential to life as God intended it.

A False Dichotomy

The story of Mary and Martha (Luke 10:38–42) has intrigued Christians through the centuries. Jesus, the rabbi from Galilee, is visiting a home of friends in Bethany, near Jerusalem. The hostess Martha is working hard to prepare the meal, and in her frustration at the lack of help goes in to complain to Jesus about her sister's negligence of duty. Jesus defends Mary, and says that her choice—to sit and listen to what he has to say—is actually the better one.

So which lifestyle is indeed better—the contemplative life or the so-called active life? The Greek philosopher Aristotle believed that contemplation was superior to rolling up your sleeves and doing things. Hundreds of years later his influence still hung over the early church, and led them to interpret the story of Mary and Martha allegorically along similar lines. Martha represented the active life, and Mary represented the contemplative. So the contemplative life—*withdrawing* from activity and responsibility to commune with God alone—was seen as Jesus' preference too. At least on this Aristotle and Jesus agreed—or so the early and then medieval church assumed. This interpretation provided the church with a biblical argument for treating the monastic life (of monks and nuns) as superior to the lifestyle of the ordinary Christian folk who struggled along in the everyday world of work and related duties.[5]

The Protestant Reformers challenged these assumptions. God designed people to do things, to live active, obedient lives that would make a difference in the world. As John Calvin said, people were created "for the express purpose of being employed in labor of various kinds, and ... no sacrifice is more pleasing to God than when every man applies diligently to his own calling, and endeavors to live in such a manner as to contribute to the general advantage."[6] The spirit of the Reformer is captured in this more contemporary statement: "We express the image of God within us, [and] we become most Godlike not when we turn away from action, but when we engage in it."[7] Relationship with God is supposed to affect how we live and act in the world.

The medieval division between the ordinary life of the Christian majority and the contemplative life of the small, spiritual elite was an unhealthy situation. Unfortunately, in too many cases the Protestant alternative shook down into a very *secular* way of life, in which there was little time or attention paid to the cultivation of a transforming personal relationship with God. We live today in a culture that is quite fixated on busyness and accomplishments. And the Protestant tradition still tends to prioritize activism. It is weaker in the relational and transformational dimensions. In any given situation, it feels natural for us to ask first, "What does God want me to be doing? Just tell me what to do and I'll do it." But it is not so easy for us to remember to ask other questions, such as: "What is God trying to *say* to me right now?" or "How does God want to craft and *shape* me through this experience?" Not just one, but all three questions need to be asked and answered.

The story of Mary and Martha was not really a showdown between the contemplative and the activist options. The story is simply a reminder of how unwise it is to squander opportunities for relationship with Christ for the sake of compulsive, wearisome, and spiritually depleting busyness. In no way does the story minimize the importance of relationally grounded practical obedience and service.

THE MONKS AT VALERYMO

Back in the sixth century, Benedict of Nursia abandoned his hermit lifestyle in order to pursue Christian spirituality in community. There he developed a community of monks atop Monte Cassino in the mountainous region of southern Italy, and wrote a basic rule to govern their life together. It exuded the wisdom of experience and the cheerfulness of grace. One of the rules Benedict laid down very early on was that a monk's life ought to reflect a daily rhythm of contemplative prayer (Latin, *ora*) and healthy work (Latin, *labora*). Benedict realized that it was neither realistic nor desirable to expect people to engage in formal prayer all the time. Life must have a rhythm to it. And so the motto of the monastic tradition became *ora et labora*— prayer *and* work.

In his bestselling novel *The Name of the Rose*, Umberto Eco provides an imaginative window into life in an Italian monastery during the Middle Ages. There is a lot going on in the monastery. Not wishing to spoil the story for anyone, let me just say that there is more going on than there should be! But Eco accurately depicts the fact that the monks did more than pray. Some labored in the kitchen with food preparation. Others had regular assignments in the town down below. And many were engaged in the monastery's chief labor—the reading and hand-copying of valuable manuscripts in the Scriptorium (that is, the library and copy center).

Most Benedictine communities welcome visitors for group or private retreats. The Benedictine community of St. Andrew's at Valerymo, up in the high desert north of Los Angeles, goes one step further and actually allows outsiders to participate with them in their daily schedule of prayers and meals. The structure of each day is built around the "hours"—the five times of corporate prayer that are spaced out from very early morning right through to the evening time.

The big bell above the chapel began to toll early one morning, echoing out across the dry brush and cactus, calling us to pray. As I stumbled bleary-eyed toward the dawn, I could see a full-figured monk, draped in a large brown robe, slowly pulling on the bell rope. Looking at the scene, it felt as though time had stopped. The picture before me was one that had hardly changed for 1,500 years—except for the large Sony headphones the monk was wearing to protect his ears from the high decibels directly overhead.

The monks at St. Andrew's operate a ceramics business. They have their own shop and kiln, and a little store you can browse or order from online. Their specialty is whimsical representations of saintly figures from the history of Christian spirituality. The saints look like oversized gingerbread cookies. Benedict and Scholastica, Francis and Clare, Hildegard of Bingen—they are all there. It's definitely not your typical retail store or factory outlet.

I was surveying the saintly samples that covered the walls like a ceramic cloud of witnesses, when I noticed a couple of monks talking in a room off to the side of the store. I called out to them: "Looks to me like this stuff required an awful lot of *labora*!" They stopped their conversation, looked over at me, and stood silent for a moment. Then one of them grinned and shot back: "Maybe so. But we still find plenty of time for *ora* too!"

Few are called to the rigorous lifestyle of a Benedictine monk, but I left Valerymo having been reminded again that *ora et labora* is the necessary rhythm of spiritual life for all of us — regardless of our station in life, our occupation in this world, or even our temperamental inclination toward introversion or extroversion. Spirituality is always about relating and being, but also about doing.

Englishman J. Hudson Taylor (1832 – 1905) comes to mind as one of countless Christian leaders through the centuries whose spirituality has been rich in all essential aspects — deeply devout, refined in character, and vigorously engaged in a worthy cause in the world. Taylor was the founding director and illustrious pioneer of the innovative and highly strategic China Inland Mission. His Christ-centered piety is described most fully in *Hudson Taylor's Spiritual Secret*, written by his son and daughter-in-law.

A THREE-DIMENSIONAL PRAYER LIFE

Prayer is a central aspect of genuine Christian spirituality. In its larger sense it is about cultivating a reverent awareness of the presence of God in all of life. An integrated spirituality — the kind we have been talking about, and want — requires a *balanced* prayer life. If we are honest, we will admit that a lot of our prayers consist of asking God to do things that we want done and delivering things we want to have. But keeping company with God involves quite a bit more than just *asking* him for things.

Richard Foster has written a wonderful book on prayer in which he identifies about twenty different kinds of prayer.[8] People are often surprised to discover that there can be so much variety in prayer. Foster divides these kinds of prayers into three categories. These categories of prayer correspond closely to our three dynamics.

In the first category, an integrated prayer life will include prayers that move *upward*, seeking intimacy with God. Included in this group are prayers of adoration, rest, meditation, and contemplation. The second category of prayers consists of those through which we look *inward*, seeking personal transformation. An integrated prayer life will include prayers of self-examination, tears, relinquishment, and formation. Prayers in the final grouping all look *outward* with others and ministry in mind: petition, intercession, authoritative prayer, and radical prayer of holy discontent with the way things are. Since all three kinds are essential to spiritual health, we need to practice them all—not just a personal favorite or two. Even our prayer life, then, should be intentionally three-dimensional.

THE CLOUD OF WITNESSES

We turn next to the great spiritual mentors of the Christian tradition. Christian spirituality is best cultivated in dialogue with godly voices from the past and present, and fortunately we are blessed with a wealth of literature from over the centuries that provides ample resources for nourishing all three dynamics. Spiritual writers reflect the assumptions of their times and places in history. Consequently, we must always use their works selectively and with discernment. It is equally worth noting how the different writers and spiritual traditions within the faith tend to emphasize different dynamics, and often give priority to one over the others.

First there are the mystical writers. These contemplative figures have left us a great legacy of insight into the nature of deep communion with God. Often they were women—like Teresa of Avila and Julian of Norwich—who responded to the gender restrictions imposed upon them by patriarchal societies by cultivating their interior life with God—to the blessing of countless men and women ever since.

Next there is the monastic tradition which has explored the transformational impulse with great passion and diligence. To the ranks of monastic figures through the centuries we would also add Protestant Puritans like John Bunyan, Richard Baxter, and John Owen; and later on John Wesley, and after him the numerous Wesleyan and Holiness leaders like Phoebe Palmer and A. B. Simpson who sought so earnestly for entire sanctification and perfect love. Into this same transformational category we can add those who have been working more recently at the intersection of Christianity and therapy to bring healing to wounded souls.

Finally, there are the mission-focused writers. These are the visionary, purpose-driven spiritual leaders whose compassion, evangelistic zeal, or demand for justice has led them to attempt great things for God in the world. The passion of their work is to be obedient in service and to do ministry in the name of Christ. Much of Pentecostal and "signs and wonders" spirituality is focused on obtaining power for effective service in this same vocational sphere.

By now you will already be anticipating the point. We must embrace the *full* scope of our spiritual heritage. We cannot afford to lock ourselves into the confines of just one stream. The mystics inspire us by their passion for God, and have much to teach us about creating space for him. But *by itself* the mystical pursuit can become self-serving and even narcissist. A different warning needs to be issued concerning the monastic or Puritan impulse. The call to holiness is central to the biblical revelation, and key to our liberation and the restoration of God's image in us. But on its own, to the neglect of everything else we have been considering, this impulse will breed legalism.[9] In the same way a fixation on mission and mission-oriented writing can have negative spiritual results. Divorced from the other two streams, it will lead to worldliness.

Each of these rivers of spirituality is rich and resourceful; by themselves they will produce imbalance and deficiencies. In order to avoid the pitfalls of narcissism, legalism, and worldliness, we need to stay in touch with the breadth of resources available to us in the Christian tradition. We also need to step beyond the confines of our respective communities, and exercise peripheral vision to scan the larger and wider landscape of Christian spirituality. For it is "together with all the Lord's people" (Ephesians 3:18) that we apprehend the fullness of God and the secrets of living well.

EVANGELICAL TENDENCIES

An interesting pattern emerges when contemporary evangelical writing on spirituality is measured against this standard. It turns out that the majority of our favorite writers gravitate toward the practical, vocational aspect of spirituality. We move most comfortably, even eagerly, into the sphere that matches our genetic predisposition as activist evangelicals. Our tradition has conditioned us to opt for the quantitative over the qualitative. We are more interested in making disciples than in being disciples—more inclined to preach the gospel than embody it. The results, unfortunately, are beginning to speak for themselves.

Historian John Webster Grant tells the story of the first efforts to evangelize the First Nations (aboriginal) peoples of western Canada. Grant got hold of the fascinating journal of a Hudson's Bay Company manager who watched Methodist James Evans competing with an equally vigorous Oblate priest for converts in the 1840s. The Protestant Evans was outstanding at his work. Yet one of his disadvantages, suggested the fur trader, was that he could barely be distinguished from the commercially preoccupied traders themselves. By contrast, the Roman Catholic priest, with his striking gown, pendulous cross, and cadaverous visage, breathed an otherworldly, spiritual air to which the Indians were much attracted.[10]

The moral is not that evangelicals should dress up as priests and look haggard. The point is that nineteenth-century Indians in western Canada had strong religious longings, and were drawn to a figure who they believed offered access to transcendent reality. Our contemporaries long for the same thing—perhaps all the more because of its relative absence in our worldly culture. Henri Nouwen reminds us that "the basis of all ministry rests ... in the mystical life."[11] And the great theologian Carl F. H. Henry observed that "the eternal realms, not one's own resources, constitute the real supply-line for genuine spirituality."[12]

In some Christian circles the reaction to excessive activism has been to turn back to the contemplative life with a vengeance. This has produced a reactionary piety that swings to the opposite extreme of social irresponsibility. And all too often, in the lurching oscillation between these two extremes, the middle theme of personal transformation falls

completely out of the picture. We are more than due for a renaissance
of holiness and healing.

We stand on the shoulders of those who have gone before us. So
we are to use the rich resources of historic Christian spirituality — but,
again, always with discernment. We should take the time to consider
the relative strengths, and deficiencies, if any, of a particular author or
book. We should look for evidence of all three spiritual dynamics, and
refuse to settle for a skewed presentation of the Christian life. Authentic spirituality never occurs automatically or merely by reading about
it. It requires that we cooperate with the Spirit's agenda by living with
disciplined intent, which is the subject of our final chapter.

-------------------- ✌ SOME HELPFUL GUIDES ✌ --------------------

THOMAS MERTON (1915 – 1968)

Merton was a cosmopolitan modern wanderer whose journey to
Christian faith is described in his now-famous autobiography *The
Seven Storey Mountain*. Thereafter he pursued his vocation as a
prolific spiritual writer within the confines of a rigorously disciplined Trappist monastery in Kentucky. The depth of Merton's
cultural awareness, and the breadth of his vision of the spiritual
life, are remarkable, and memorably expressed in such classics as
No Man Is an Island and *New Seeds of Contemplation*.

RICHARD FOSTER

Foster has done more perhaps than anyone else to introduce contemporaries to the rich and varied resources of classic Christian
spirituality. He has carefully mined these resources and made
them accessible to a large audience today. Among Foster's many
important and integrative publications are his study of *Prayer*,
a coedited volume of *Devotional Classics*, and *Streams of Living
Water: Celebrating the Great Traditions of Christian Faith*. He is
also founder of Renovaré ministries.

DALLAS WILLARD

Dallas Willard is a professor of philosophy at the University of Southern California whose contribution to spirituality parallels that of Oxford scholar C. S. Lewis's contribution to apologetics. Willard's trilogy of *Hearing God*, *Renovation of the Heart*, and *The Divine Conspiracy* roughly parallels the three dimensions of spirituality presented in this volume. These books are distributed throughout our concluding bibliography according to their respective emphases. When taken together, they offer an integrated vision of the Christian life.

CHAPTER SUMMARY

Each of us should seek to live a Christ-centered, Spirit-filled life characterized by all three dynamics of Christian spirituality. These dynamics are linked together, dependent on one another, and equally important to our spiritual health. Christ calls us to experience them, and the Holy Spirit intentionally nurtures them in us. We should consciously incorporate all three into our prayer lives as well. Evangelicals especially need to be aware that an undue fixation on the vocational can drift toward functional secularism. The classics of Christian spirituality offer rich resources to be accessed with discernment. By measuring them against this three-dimensional standard, we can appreciate their insights while recognizing possible weaknesses and oversights.

LIVING WITH DISCIPLINED INTENT

Be diligent in these matters; give yourself wholly to them.

1 Timothy 4:15

A north-south line of impressive buildings and public spaces runs right through the heart of Beijing. This central axis of Chinese history and culture includes the Forbidden City, for centuries the fortified palatial residence of China's emperors. The temple of Shangdi, the Supreme God of ancient Chinese religion, is also here. That temple has been of such significance to China that it survived even the Cultural Revolution's wholesale assault on religious faith. And then there is Tiananmen Square, the vast central gathering place of the new People's Republic of China.

I arrived at the square at dusk one evening. A soldier stood guard at a flagpole as a large crowd of patriotic Chinese gathered for the lowering of the flag at day's end. At one end of Tiananmen, in the distance, Chairman Mao Zedong's body lay in state. And high on a tile-roofed red wall, along the opposite side of the square just above us, hung his massive portrait. In a nation of over a billion citizens, this man stands alone. His name and picture have become synonymous with China.

Gazing on this memorial to China's revolutionary hero, my thoughts turned to another Chinese citizen whose greatness is largely overlooked on the world stage. Somewhere in the surrounding drab sprawl of low-budget, weather-stained apartments an elderly Chinese man lived out his final days in relative obscurity. At one time Wang Mingdao (1901 – 1991) was one of China's most prominent preachers. Like so many other believers in this vast nation, he was persecuted by the Communists who came to power in the revolutionary victory of 1949, for his adamant refusal to acknowledge the government's authority over the church. He was imprisoned and subjected during his jail time to intense, unrelenting ideological and psychological abuse. Eventually, in 1956, this Christian leader (nicknamed "Iron Wang" for his lifelong toughness) broke down, confessed his "errors," and renounced his convictions. He was released a broken man. By all accounts the atheist government had prevailed.[1]

But it was not the end for Wang Mingdao. Overcome with remorse, he claimed the grace of God's forgiveness and renounced the compromises he had previously made. He rebounded like Lazarus from the grave. Promptly rearrested, he and his wife Jingwen were sent back to prison for years to come. But this time he was resilient. He suffered greatly until his release as an old man in 1979. Not all Chinese Christians supported Wang's convictions, but his defiance of the secular powers was a powerful inspiration to the rapidly growing Chinese house church movement of the twentieth century. His life is a challenge to be faithful to the calling we receive, not necessarily the calling we might choose — and that faithfulness is not always easy. Yet the discipline of being faithful will make us, like it made Wang Mingdao, changed people.

The Longest Journey

North Americans are great travelers. The long journey is central to our national mythologies. We celebrate Lewis and Clark's expedition and the heroics of the pioneers' Oregon Trail. The mystique of the journey is preserved on old Route 66 today, as well as on the

Trans-Canada highway to the north. Novelists like John Steinbeck, in *Grapes of Wrath* and *Travels with Charley*, have captured this ethos, while popular songs celebrate the freedom of the open road.

Journeys or pilgrimages are also central themes in the Bible. Abraham followed the call of God and set out in obedience from his hometown on the Euphrates. He lived in tents and journeyed all his life. His descendents escaped from slavery in Egypt, squeezing through a water-walled canyon in the Red Sea. Their exodus journey became the central metaphor of salvation. And in the centuries that followed, their devout descendents, their hearts set on pilgrimage, rallied annually in Jerusalem to celebrate the high festivals together (Psalm 84:5).

Jesus never invited his disciples to adopt a comfortable sitting position for long. His call was to movement, to *follow* him. The apostle Paul saw the Christian life this way as well. "Forgetting what is behind and straining toward what is ahead," he said, "I press on toward the goal to win the prize for which God has called me heavenward in Christ Jesus" (Philippians 3:13–14). Calling them to do the same, he urged believers to *keep in step* with the Spirit.

The most important journey a Christian takes is not one that crosses geographic territory. It is, rather, an inward journey—the journey from head to heart. It is the journey from knowledge to experience, from a merely cognitive awareness of truth to its deep actualization in our relationships, our souls, and the ways we invest our lives. This is where, as we say, the rubber meets the road. Donald Coggin, a former archbishop of Canterbury, put the challenge succinctly when he noted that "the journey from head to heart is one of the longest and most difficult we know."[2]

I cannot think of a single giant of Christian spirituality who would disagree with this. John Calvin was a theologian of prodigious intellect. In his *Institutes of the Christian Religion*, the premier theology textbook of the Reformation, he acknowledged that truth must never be allowed to merely flit about in the brain. It must take deep root in the soul. Likewise Ignatius of Loyola, at the beginning of his *Spiritual Exercises*, reminds his readers that "what fills and satisfies the soul consists, not in knowing much, but in our understanding the realities *profoundly* and in savoring them *interiorly*."[3]

So far this book has been largely informational. It has provided a way of seeing the topic. We have been trying to make sense out of what the Christian life is all about. However, the goal of Christian spirituality lies beyond *understanding* what it means to live all of life before God. That is only a means to an end. The higher goal is to *experience* these things in our lives. Understanding the dynamics of Christian spirituality gives us something to aim for, and that's a good start. But it is only a start. We need to make real progress toward the goal.

There are many ways to make coffee. We usually prepare ours by dripping hot water through a cone-shaped coffee filter. But recently one of our daughters gave us a new gadget for Christmas: a coffee-maker that uses a plunger (the official name is a French press). It pushes fresh-ground coffee forcibly down through boiling hot water. The result is a rich coffee brew—arguably the best there is.

That's a lot like it has to be with the truths of the spiritual life. They have to be pressed down hard into our hearts in such a way that things really do become new and different. Otherwise, our experience will remain thin and weak, barely changed at all, and lacking the telltale aroma of God. Truth must be pushed down until it becomes internalized, deeply rooted in the soil of the soul, shaping our habits and involuntary responses, and altering the default settings of our psyches.

MORE THAN AN OPTION

We have to start thinking about spirituality in a new way. The problem is that frequently it is regarded as an *option* for believers. It is considered a good thing (like apple pie, the flag, and motherhood), especially for some, but less than necessary for everyone. It is welcomed as a healthy pursuit for a subset of Christians who happen to be so inclined. Correcting this misperception is crucial.

We have not wanted to say that salvation (used as a code word for guaranteed admission to heaven) depends on conscientiously applying ourselves to living a spiritual life. Sometimes evangelicals commend spirituality by stressing the credibility and power that godly lives provide for the church's task of witness. All too often church leaders will, out of sheer frustration, try to promote spirituality by making negligent Christians feel guilty and ashamed of themselves.

The problem is that none of the dynamics of Christian spirituality touches directly what popular evangelicalism assumes are the mechanics of getting and staying saved. The heart of salvation is thought to be justification by faith alone, by means of which sinners acquire guaranteed eternal life. Ultimately, then, salvation is a matter of position and status. Everything else is optional icing on the cake. There is a better way. It starts with realizing that our salvation involves more than a *legal* transaction. We certainly should celebrate justification by faith alone. This is a gospel truth that frees our hearts and gives us confidence before God. But we subvert authentic spirituality when we make justification by faith (which is a transactional concept) central to our understanding of the Christian life.[4]

We need to see that justification is one aspect of something even more central—our supernatural union with Christ through the Spirit's work in our lives.[5] From this perspective, indifference to the divine impulses flowing into our lives can be seen for the perilous activity it really is. Ignoring or thwarting these impulses of God's Spirit in our hearts will only undermine and retard his saving activity in our lives.

Obviously salvation in the New Testament sense is about more than *future* blessings. Salvation in the fullest sense is God's determined campaign to deliver us from the power and effects of sin—a campaign that is *already* underway. It is supposed to begin making a positive difference right away. As a result of our union with Christ, God's life begins flowing into our own, and the process of salvation— God's resolute campaign to deliver us from the power and effects of sin—is launched *here and now.*

A PASSION FOR SPIRITUALITY

The mystical town of Assisi exudes a transcendent spirit as it rises above the fertile plain of Umbria. Now one of the holiest sites in Christendom, it was here that Francis (1182–1226), the privileged son of a wealthy local merchant, once lived, played, and fought alongside his friends. But one day, as a young adult, he had a powerful vision of God and chose to pursue his new call with his whole heart. He had a charismatic personality—a natural gift of leadership—and before long a zealous band of friends and peers had rallied around him to form what became the Franciscan order.

Francis's extravagant generosity toward the poor put him on a collision course with his exasperated father, who feared that the family assets were being squandered. Climbing up through the steep cobblestone paths of Assisi one day, puffing for breath as I did, I thought about the day, almost a millennium earlier, when Francis publicly renounced his family wealth. He had chosen, in his dramatic way, to disrobe completely, and stand naked in the town square as a public declaration of his resolve to give up *everything* to pursue God and his ways. From then on he and his associates had humbly to beg for their food and basic needs as they cheerfully served others.

This was the beginning of a radical discipleship that changed the face of the medieval church. The passion for God of Francis of Assisi, Wang Mingdao, and others like them, challenges us. We are reminded that authentic spirituality is often costly and countercultural, for it requires that we keep ourselves "from being polluted by the world" (James 1:27). We have to be prepared to live as resident aliens. Perhaps it is time for a new monasticism—a fresh way of living in resistance to the toxic influences of mainstream culture.

My wife and I began to think about studying in Scotland while we lived in Canada. The more we talked about it, the more it became a shared dream. Eventually some tough decisions had to be made. Kate was pregnant. We had considered using our modest savings to make a down payment on a house in Vancouver's rising real estate market, but decided in the end to put it all into our overseas study fund. We also shoveled in a little sentimental inheritance left to us by a great-aunt. In response to prudent critics, we announced with bravado that we were prepared, if necessary, to rent forever.

Then we sold our car—and I remember actually crying as the new owner drove it away. Left with a few pieces of luggage, we headed for the airport and our transatlantic flight. For the next three years we either walked or took the bus wherever we went. We declined a phone, and saved by using the coin-operated one down the street. We gave up relatively expensive hamburger meat for a steady diet of omelets, and celebrated our anniversary by sharing a can of Coca-Cola. We were financially strapped, but we were living our dream.

After a year, we flew back home to show off our little newborn daughter to grandparents and extended family. One night we were having dinner with some friends. He had a great job as a corporate executive. Their new home was huge and elegantly decorated. There was a luxury car in the garage and a nice van in the driveway. Over dessert my friend turned and said, "We'd give everything to do what you guys are doing." It was great to hear our big decision validated by a friend. But I couldn't help thinking to myself: "Interesting—that's *exactly* what it's costing us."

Everything has its price. And church history suggests that the spiritual life is no exception. Dissatisfaction with mainstream life can lead some to despair, but for others it can be a stimulus toward a radically different set of priorities. The spiritual journey from head to heart requires a passion for the real thing. It's hard, Jesus said, for those who are rich—for those who are already comfortable (Matthew 19:23). There is a future, however, for anyone who is willing, if called upon, to give up everything.

How deeply do we want to experience authentic spirituality? How high a priority is it going to be for us? Life has a curious way of delivering what really means the most to us. The obituary someone will read at my funeral will reflect the things that were most important to me while I lived. If this is so, we can see what A. W. Tozer meant when he claimed that each one of us is as spiritual as we really want to be.

CREATING SPACE FOR GOD

This is where *disciplined intent* comes in. Neither our natural dispositions nor the contemporary environment is conducive to the cultivation of the spiritual life. Thus *discipline* becomes so important—the business of firmly resisting and restraining these powerful negative forces in our lives. As Dallas Willard forcefully insists, "Grace is not opposed to *effort*; it is opposed to *earning*." [6] It is a distinction definitely worth pondering.

It is true that our salvation can never be earned. But too many have mistakenly assumed that because grace is free, no exertion is required of us to live the Christian life. This is simply untrue. We are called to participate with all our hearts in the purposes of God for us and the world. Precisely because God is already at work in us, we are to work out our salvation with fear and trembling (Philippians 2:12–13).

Living with disciplined intent must begin with creating space for God.[7] We cannot unilaterally create or demand a relationship with him, but we can optimally position ourselves as welcoming toward him. We can realign our priorities. We can clear out some of the clutter, the inane and relentless busyness, the distractions—the layers of superficiality that get in the road of authentic life in the Spirit. We can never, of course, *make* God come and renew us. We can only extend our heartfelt welcome and wait. Yet we can do so with patient anticipation, knowing that he desires relationship as well.

Reaching up in a posture of invitation requires that we practice the Sabbath principle. Strict observance of the Sabbath day (Saturday) is obsolete now for Christians, but the value of a day of common pause (traditionally, Sunday) continues, and the Sabbath "principle" (which is not tied to a weekly calendar at all) is certainly still in effect. Our world today is not very hospitable to cultivating life in the Spirit. It is easy to underestimate how seductive the social environment is, and the ways it keeps us distracted from the truly important issues of life. Sadly, many are moving toward eternity without appropriate focus on what is really important.

Jesus accepted the rhythms of human life before God, as he paused to reconnect, be renewed, and regain perspective. We must learn again to be still and attentive. It is a discipline of faith to trust that our needs will be taken care of, even if we pause for a moment and allow the competition to run ahead. Yet there are such compensating benefits to setting aside our secular activism, withdrawing from our otherwise hypercaffeinated existence, and choosing to live the Sabbath principle before God.[8]

KINDS OF SPACE

There are at least three kinds of space we can create for God. The first is *chronological space*—setting aside the time necessary for relationship to God and the experience of his renewing touch and guiding command. This is difficult to create, because our lives are already full. Often it takes something drastic, like an illness—putting us flat on our backs—or losing our jobs, to slow us down. Otherwise, every moment is filled with what can be easily justified as useful and necessary activity. Our first reaction is to create space by cranking up the intensity of our lives one more notch, to inject just a bit more caffeine into things. It is like adding more pounds of air pressure to a fully inflated tire. The only real solution comes through relinquishment. We have to decide what we will give up in order to create chronological space. Something has to be subtracted. This is the hardest, but perhaps the most important, aspect of the matter.

The second kind of space we need to carve out is *psychological* space. It is pointless to set aside time for God if other things continue to dominate our consciousness and distract us from the relationship at hand. It is not enough to sit down to pray, if our mind just floods with items on our to-do list. I can recall one of my theology professors years ago explaining, with respect to worship, that it is not enough to attend church on Sunday morning. We also needed to get to bed at a reasonable hour on Saturday night so that we might enter into Sunday worship with a clear, well-rested, and focused consciousness. That is just one example of how psychological space is created.

The third variety is *physical* space. We are earthlings, tethered to this planet, and our physical location affects our lives with God. We cannot engage very well in extended prayer with the television on. We cannot hope to get very far if we feel compelled to answer our incoming cell phone calls. I know a harried mother of young children whose only escape from the incessant demands of the home is to hide for short spaces of time in the darkness of her bedroom closet. There she connects with God.

Some of us may find a particular environment—whether that is outdoors with nature, or in a church rich in symbols and beauty—conducive to communing with God. Others have a special place they return to for important times of prayer—a particular chair near the window, under a favorite Ponderosa pine on a cliff overlooking the ocean, or whatever. They find that doing so helps them to center in on their relationship with God. It requires self-discipline, adjusted priorities, and relinquishment of old habits to create space for God. It is difficult to make the necessary changes, but great is the benefit of stepping off the treadmill and attending to things that matter most.

READING THE BIBLE *Slowly*

The evangelical tradition is Bible-centered, and the daily "quiet time," for personal Bible reading and prayer, is perhaps its quintessential spiritual discipline. For this reason, something needs to be said about the meditative use of the Christian Scriptures as an aid to spirituality.[9] We must learn to read the Bible in a way that nourishes all three of its dynamics.

Christians have worked hard to develop responsible approaches to Bible study. We have adopted historical-grammatical methods for interpreting Scripture correctly. And over the years we have employed a rather sophisticated apparatus of scholarly tools to help us. Our goal has been to discover truth, not to invent it. Yet despite its positive achievements, the historical-grammatical methods of biblical scholarship *by themselves* have not served the church as well as one might hope. They can actually damage the vitality of the church because of their deficiencies in facilitating three things: encounter with God, personal formation, and practical application. To paraphrase the handwriting on the wall of King Belshazzar's Babylonian palace, they have been weighed on the scales and found wanting.

The spiritual instincts of the people of God cannot be satisfied with an approach to the Bible that fails to connect readers directly with God, minimizes personal formation, and fades out when it comes to making practical applications. Fortunately, there is an alternative approach, which is not new but rather a resuscitation of a venerable tradition of encountering the Word. This approach goes by a number of names, including a meditative approach to Scripture or the spiritual reading of the Bible.

The comedian Woody Allen tells the story of how he learned to speed-read. Having taken the training, he tried out his news skills on Leo Tolstoy's novel *War and Peace*. Allen breezed through the massive tome in about thirty seconds. Looking up afterward, he reported on what he had gleaned. "It's about Russia," he said. By contrast, the spiritual reading approach to the Bible, which emerged early on in the history of Christianity in the Benedictine tradition of *lectio divina* (literally, divine reading), is characterized by unhurried, reflective consideration. It is about the *slow* reading of Scripture.

Through its posture of silent, attentive listening, the meditative approach to Scripture opens the reader up to the quiet voice of God. It sets a tone of humility and receptivity, rather than one of assertiveness and control. Dietrich Bonhoeffer, the German martyr, like many others, commended this approach. He claimed that it was the best way to wait for the Word to address us personally. In *Life Together*, his little classic on Christian community, Bonhoeffer warned against neglecting to listen for the living voice of God. The obscene alternative is just to prattle on in God's neglected presence.[10] The Bible is a repository of God's past communication, and where God has already spoken is a logical place to look for him to continue to speak.

Meditating on Scripture makes sense for another reason. It helps us internalize its truth. The goal is not to discover new thoughts, but to allow familiar or neglected ones to penetrate our hearts. So the literature on spiritual reading is full of imagery of slow rumination. The *Anglican Prayer Book* includes a prayer that we may "inwardly digest" God's Word. We do not always find this easy. It is a radical suggestion "for us to read to be formed and transformed rather than to gather information. We are information seekers. We love to cover territory."[11]

Finally, meditation on Scripture creates a context in which it is possible to develop creative connections between the text and our own immediate life situation. This dovetails with an emerging awareness these days that the significance of a particular Scripture is not so much embedded in the text by itself as it is discovered in the interplay between the inspired text and the reader's own reality—in other words, in the dynamic intersection between some inspired ancient writing and the things that are happening in the reader's situation right now. And if our imaginations have been thoroughly "baptized" in the larger truth structure of Scripture, we will have a firewall against misleading subjectivity.

Again it was Bonhoeffer who forcefully criticized the common way in which sermon-building preachers deflect away the pointed message of the Bible from themselves. "Do not ask how you should tell it to others," he urges, "but ask what it tells *you*."[12] It is important, therefore, to keep from reading only for information, or merely to perform official ministry duties. Otherwise it is almost impossible to listen to what God may be saying to *us*. The linkage between what a text, composed perhaps thousands of years ago in the ancient Near East, meant at the time, and what it now signifies in our personal situation today, is not according to some straightforward logical circuitry. It is not simply a matter of connecting the dots. We need the Spirit's guidance as we venture beyond the text's historical context to its present-day application to us. The spiritual reading of Scripture addresses this.

The spiritually expectant approach to Scripture which I have been commending has long been celebrated in our songs of worship. For example, in the hymn *Break Thou the Bread of Life*, Mary Lathbury and Alexander Groves wrote: "Beyond the sacred page, I see thee, Lord; my spirit pants for thee, O Living Word."[13] This lyrical phrase expresses very well the pattern of going to the Word, not as an end in itself, but so that through it we might connect with God, his transforming touch, and guiding voice.

THE CLASSIC SPIRITUAL DISCIPLINES

Spiritual disciplines are time-honored practices that help us create space for God, internalize his truth, and obey him with courage and consistency. The disciplines are not self-improvement techniques. Rather, they are ways in which we try to cooperate with the movement of the Spirit in our lives. Perhaps a tiny bit of pastoral advice is appropriate here. We must each find out which disciplines work best for us as unique individuals. This is not the same as saying that everyone should gravitate to what they find *easiest*. Often God challenges us at the points of our weakness. But we should be attentive to which disciplines seem to be most satisfying and *fruitful* for us as individuals. And secondly, we should not be so ambitious as to set ourselves up for failure. It is better to attempt baby steps than giant leaps forward. And try not to be too hard on yourself when your mortality shows. Remember, as a follower of Jesus you were invited to join a religion totally marinated in grace.

Many outstanding resources dealing with the spiritual disciplines—a lavish number, really—are available to us today. Even if it were desirable, it would be impossible to summarize here all the insights they contain. It will be enough to note that they start with a firm resolve to take advantage of the "means of grace"—by engaging in consistent prayer, meditating on Scripture, listening to the Word preached with integrity, accessing the ordinances (or, sacraments) of the church, regularly confessing one's sins, singing edifying songs and hymns, and joining regularly with other believers in worship, fellowship, and service.

There are a myriad of classic disciplines as well. There is meditation, contemplation, self-examination and confession, fasting, journaling, retreats, and simplicity—to list just some. All these disciplines share some common purposes. They make us more attentive to the presence and leading of God. They allow God's truth to take deep and enduring root in our souls. Like the plunger in a French coffeemaker, they push it down from our heads into our hearts, and out from there to guide our hands and feet.

Some disciplines address in a special way our chronic struggle with the inward curve of our human natures. They help us open up space for other people in our lives. They are medicine for our predisposition toward self-absorption. Hospitality and neighborliness (1 Peter 4:9; Luke 10:25–37) are two important examples. The discipline of generosity (1 Timothy 6:18), which also enlarges our hearts and widens our horizons, is another.

These spiritual disciplines include the accessing of spiritual directors, mentors, and friends. Soul-friendships are special gifts, for to them, David Benner explains, I am able to "bring my whole self, especially my inner self."[14] It is humbling (in a healthy sense) to discover how much our spiritual lives are dependent upon, and enriched by, the contributions of others. Augustine understood very clearly the communal nature of Christian existence: "Shared was our loss," he explained, and "shared be our finding."[15] We fell together and we will recover together. His ideal for Christian community was summed up in an eloquent phrase: "One soul and one heart intent upon God."[16]

Finally, there will be a place for developing a personal "rule of life."[17] After growing in self-understanding, listening to godly mentors, and weighing the deepest desires of our heart, it is appropriate to establish a flexible yet intentional plan of action for the cultivation of spirituality. This is the discipline of a personal rule.

There is freedom here to choose what is most compatible with your own temperament and inclinations. Some, for example, may find that fasting brings clarity, while for others only fatigue. Depending on our makeup, music may or may not figure large in our personal rule. Connecting with God's creation will be more soul-nourishing for some than for others. We will be drawn, to a greater or lesser extent, to the power of liturgy, symbolism, and even architectural settings. We all require companionship and solitude, but we will gravitate to different mixtures of these essential ingredients. There is freedom here.

THE UNEXPECTED DISCIPLINES

So far we have been considering the classic spiritual disciplines. Sometimes the discipline God allows into our lives is highly individualized, and is determined by our unique circumstances. We may sustain injuries in a traffic accident, lose our job, or become obliged to care for an aging, invalid relative. We should not curse these events as bad luck, or become embittered by them. Even through such highly undesirable experiences, the dynamics of Christian spirituality can flourish in new ways. In all such forms of suffering God is still compassionately at work—salvaging good for those who love him (Romans 8:28). These unique circumstantial disciplines function as refining fires that produce qualities of enduring value to God's glory. Their ultimate purpose is to see the relational disposition, moral character, and purposeful actions of Christ mirrored in his resilient followers.

With this we conclude our little guide to Christian spirituality. God has invited us to experience the fullness of all this by living our lives, as Wang Mingdao lived his, with disciplined intent. A great deal hinges on our response to God's invitation to do so.

———————————— ✐ SOME HELPFUL GUIDES ✐ ————————

FRANCIS DE SALES (1567 – 1622)

Francis de Sales, who was introduced earlier in this volume, was a leader in a spiritual renewal movement that emerged as a counterpoint to the often-violent post-Reformation religious conflicts in Europe. He wrote a treatise *On the Love of God*, which explored what it means to love God fervently. But his most significant legacy has been the enduring classic *Introduction to the Devout Life*. In it he offers many doable spiritual exercises that appeal to the mind, the emotions, and the will as means of internalizing truth.

JOHN (1703 – 1791) AND CHARLES (1707 – 1788) WESLEY

The Wesley brothers were leaders in the Great Awakening and cofounders of Methodism. John remains an inspirational example by his joyfully disciplined life, attentiveness to formation in small groups ("classes"), and tireless efforts in outreach and practical service. The many hymns and songs of his brother Charles embody and perpetuate his teachings—a reminder of the unique power of music in Christian spirituality. The Wesley legacy is accessible through good biographies and volumes of selected writings, and by browsing just about any Christian hymnal in the world.

MARJORIE THOMPSON

Marjorie Thompson studied spirituality with Henri Nouwen at Yale. Her book *Soul Feast* is an eloquently written and aesthetically presented invitation to the privileges and disciplines of the spiritual life—one of the very best available. She is a frequent contributor to *Weavings*, a journal of the spiritual life. An ordained Presbyterian minister, she serves with the Upper Room ministry in Nashville, Tennessee, and there lives out her commitment to cultivating family and congregational spirituality through publishing and speaking.

CHAPTER SUMMARY

This chapter explored the challenging journey from knowledge to experience — a journey the Spirit wants us, and encourages us, to take. It must begin and be sustained by a passion for the things of God. It then requires creating space for God in our distracted lives. Our temperament will be a factor in determining the specific mix of contemplation and activity that is best for us, but in general we all need to resist the hyperactive and superficial tendencies of contemporary culture. Spiritual disciplines are time-honored practices that help us create space for God, internalize his transforming truth, and experience his guidance and strength in our lives.

YEARNING FOR BETTER DAYS

Come, Lord Jesus.
Revelation 22:20

Old Jerusalem contains a wall that is sacred to the Jews. Built of large stone blocks, it serves as a retaining foundation on the west side of the ancient site now occupied by a famous Muslim mosque. This wall may be the only surviving vestige of the last Jewish temple, the one built by Herod before the time of Christ, and long since demolished by a Roman army. Here Jews come to pray, with prayer shawls draped across their shoulders, and sometimes little boxes of Torah strapped to their foreheads. Some people write their petitions on scraps of paper and stuff them into cracks in the mortar. Those more conservative among them wear long beards and black broad-brimmed hats. They rock back and forth in motions of supplication, crying out to God to deliver on his long-standing promises of messianic protection, justice, and national *shalom*.

It is a poignant and moving scene. More than anything else it exudes an atmosphere of *yearning*—of longing for things greatly desired but so long deferred. The cry going up in a myriad of languages is essentially the same one: "How long, O Lord, how long?" A friend and I stood at the wall one day, touching the cold stone with our fingers, soaking up the ancient ethos, and feeling the pulse of the Jewish faith. A stooped-over old man with an unkempt white beard suspended his prayers and shuffled over to us. He looked up at us through sad, watery eyes, and in halting English inquired whether we were Jewish. We told him we were not. It was clear as he slowly moved off that our answer had disappointed him.

I wanted to call out after him: "You're not the only ones who know the agony of having to wait, you know. You're not alone in *yearning* for better days long overdue. What we Christians, who have put our hope in Jesus, feel in our hearts isn't altogether different from what you are feeling." Yes, there's an incomplete dimension to our existence as well. Whether we wait for the Messiah's first or second coming, the visceral emotion waiting generates is much the same. This is certainly true in the sphere of our spirituality. The relational, transformational, and vocational dynamics of the Christian life are real and may be experienced in satisfying ways. Yet we set ourselves up for disillusionment by expecting more than can be delivered in this fallen world of ours.

There are moments when we catch direct glimpses of the Father's heart and experience the sweet joy of being in loving covenant with him.[1] But there are other, darker times when there is no *affect* at all, only silence, and a slithering whisper that this was all made up, and we really *are* alone. There are moments when the body of Christ feels like the best family ever, and there are other times when all its hurtful dysfunctions push us to the very edge of cynicism.

We will struggle with our narcissist natures all our lives— wounding and being wounded in ways that put friendships and family ties at risk. We will never get beyond temptation to a point where it will be safe to drop our guard. We will need to keep dipping into the reservoir of God's forgiveness and taking advantage of the gracious forbearance of others. We are all persons with disabilities, limping our way back to God.

And it is not always easy to discern the will of God in the complex circumstances of our lives. Some of our hard work for his sake will bear the marks of missteps and end up looking rather futile. People to whom we have given our lives may not seem particularly appreciative of our investment. Sometimes our legacy may seem more like a sand castle, tediously constructed under the hot sun, only to be swept away by the incoming tide of unforeseen circumstances or a new administration with a different vision.

The journey to the Celestial City can be every bit as arduous as John Bunyan depicted in his famous *Pilgrim's Progress*. It will not always be filled with happy faces, fun times, and an incessant fare of upbeat praise choruses. There will be tears too, and through it all the ache of yearning. We face into the wind as we journey through this fallen world, and there are plenty of struggles ahead. Nowhere does the Bible say it will be easy. We have only been assured that it is infinitely worthwhile.

But we also journey in hope, and by hope we mean a confident and sustaining anticipation of a positive future. We have received sufficient assurances that we are on the right track (traveling mercies, Anne Lamott calls them) to keep us pressing forward. It is true that for the time being we know only "in part." But someday we *will* see him face-to-face, and will know him fully, just as we are already fully known (1 Corinthians 13:12). The time is coming when we will "slip the surly bonds of earth ... and touch the face of God."[2]

Likewise our progress toward holiness and wholeness is partial at best, but we look ahead to when we will finally be like him, and every tear will be wiped away. And we count on that promised day when we will sit down to a great banquet celebrating the full and final victory of the reign of God. And at that banquet the secret will be disclosed of how our modest labors for this cause were not in vain.

As we move toward this destiny, sustained by the power of the Spirit, we must keep praying as Jesus taught us to pray (Matthew 6:9–13). "*Our Father* in heaven" — here, right up front, is an acknowledgment of the intimate familial relationship that needs to set the emotional atmosphere for everything that follows. "Hallowed be your name" is essentially a prayer for our transformation, since God's name will be respected to the extent that our character and conduct, as people bearing his name, bring him honor rather than reproach.[3]

And finally, "your kingdom come" is a reminder that God's great and overarching plan to bless the world is the thing of paramount importance, and we discover our greatest joy and meaning by contributing to it. This is the foundation for everything else that follows. Living out the spirit of this classic Jesus-style prayer *is* authentic Christian spirituality. Every pilgrimage is unique, yet in these perennial ways all our journeys are the same.

ENCOURAGEMENT FOR THE JOURNEY

Perhaps you are wondering what to do next. The previous chapter offered some suggestions, but there is really no "one size fits all" plan. In Bunyan's classic, *Pilgrim's Progress*, Evangelist meets Christian, who is wandering through the fields without a sense of direction. His role is to point the bewildered pilgrim toward his true destination. But he does not provide a detailed itinerary with all the right and left turns printed out in advance. It is Christian's journey, and he must choose his own steps.

"Do you see yonder shining light?" Evangelist asks.

"I think I do," replies Christian, squinting at the horizon.

"Keep that light in your eye," says Evangelist. Then, urging him forward, he assures Christian that as he gets closer, he will be told what to do next.[4]

And that's pretty much the way it works.

We have young adult daughters moving out of the nest these days. As they drive off, their backseats stuffed with clothes and CDs, we assure them of our love, wave wistfully, and shout salvos of parental encouragement and advice. Sometimes I imagine Evangelist doing the same for Christian. In my mind's eye I see him cupping his hands around his mouth to project his voice toward the figure disappearing over the hill. And the advice he offers Christian echoes scriptural truth and the accumulated wisdom of God's people through the centuries. On the wind I catch phrases like these ...

Never forget that our culture is a vast conspiracy
to distract you from the real point of living.
All is lost if you simply go with the flow.

Decide what you really—I mean really—
want most out of life, because chances are
that's what you'll end up getting.

Remember that your Father in heaven
loves you and wills your happiness.

Delight in God and be hospitable to his Spirit.

Always be attentive.

Be faithful in relationships.

Marinate your mind in the truth and
let it alter the default settings of your psyche.

Dare to be honest, especially with yourself.

Regularly claim God's forgiveness through Christ,
then refuse to wallow in guilt feelings.

Cultivate a taste for the good.

Find godly mentors and sacred companions.

Submit to God's will and do so without whining.

Be brave in your obedience and take risks.

Stay resilient in adversity.

Live expectantly.

See your life as the great gift it is —
and be thankful for it.

View all this as a brief prelude
to a wondrous eternity.

Sing, even through your tears.

And may the Lord bless you
and keep you . . .

Questions for Individual and Group Reflection

Chapter 1: Getting Started

1. What is generic spirituality all about?
2. What makes Christian spirituality unique and distinctive?
3. How would you explain its three dynamics to a friend?
4. In which of these dimensions of Christian spirituality do you sense your own greatest need and desire to grow?

Chapter 2: Friendship with God

1. Why is the possibility of a relationship with God so appealing?
2. What are some major obstacles to developing a deep one?
3. In what ways, if any, do you wish to reshape your perception of God?
4. What all is involved in being a friend of God?

Chapter 3: Experiencing Community

1. What is the natural connection between love for God and love for others?
2. Why is it so hard to forgive and start over?
3. Share an experience of community that seemed to be a work of the Holy Spirit.
4. What, if anything, do you sense God saying to you about this topic?

Chapter 4: The Renewal of Holiness

1. What is holiness and why is it more a gift than a duty?
2. Discuss the place of honesty and authenticity in moral transformation.

3. How should we properly interpret the biblical invitations to "crucifixion"?

4. What about all this do you find confusing? What have you found helpful?

Chapter 5: The Healing of Our Wounds

1. What are the chief causes of our woundedness? And why is it important to distinguish them from one another?

2. What wounds sadden and concern you the most as you observe human life?

3. Prove from Scripture that God is involved in both physical and inner healing.

4. Why is the concept of "wounded healer" both bad news and good news?

Chapter 6: Discovering Purpose and Meaning

1. What does it mean to have a vocation?

2. How is this different from the secular quest for personal fulfillment?

3. If we are saved by grace, not by works, why should we be interested in the vocational dynamic?

4. Will pastors and missionaries have more purpose and meaning in their lives than laypersons? Explain.

Chapter 7: The Gift of a Personal Calling

1. How does God treat us as adults as we seek his personal calling in our lives?

2. Why is it freeing to see ourselves as team members in the family of God?

3. What do you think of Frederick Buechner's advice on how to locate one's personal calling in life?

4. Which is most needed in the matter of a personal call — discernment or courage?

CHAPTER 8: AN INTEGRATED SPIRITUALITY

1. Give examples of ways the Holy Spirit actively encourages all three dynamics.
2. How do healthy transformational and vocational dynamics rebound to enrich our relationship with God through Christ?
3. What can we all learn from the Benedictine motto of *ora et labora*?
4. In pursuit of an integrated spirituality, which dynamic(s) do you desire to give a higher priority in your prayers and reading choices?

CHAPTER 9: LIVING WITH DISCIPLINED INTENT

1. Does meditative prayer sound inviting or intimidating to you? Why?
2. Share something that happened while you were *slowly* reading Scripture.
3. Which truths from this book do you want to take deep root in your heart?
4. What will be your new plan as you return to your normal life routines and responsibilities?

Going Deeper: Resources for Further Study

General Resources

Chan, Simon. *Spiritual Theology*. Downers Grove, Ill.: InterVarsity Press, 1998.

Collins, Kenneth, ed. *Exploring Christian Spirituality*. Grand Rapids, Mich.: Baker, 2000.

Cunningham, Lawrence and Keith Egan. *Christian Spirituality: Themes from the Tradition*. New York and Mahwah, N.J.: Paulist Press, 1996.

George, Timothy and Alister McGrath, eds. *For All the Saints: Evangelical Theology and Christian Spirituality*. Louisville, Ky.: Westminster John Knox, 2003.

Packer, J. I. and Loren Wilkinson, eds. *Alive to God: Studies in Spirituality*. Downers Grove, Ill.: InterVarsity Press, 1992.

Peterson, Eugene. *Christ Plays in Ten Thousand Places: A Conversation in Spiritual Theology*. Grand Rapids, Mich.: Eerdmans, 2005.

Rienstra, Debra. *So Much More: An Invitation to Christian Spirituality*. San Francisco: Jossey-Bass, 2005.

Sheldrake, Philip, ed. *New Westminster Dictionary of Christian Spirituality*. Louisville, Ky.: Westminster John Knox, 2005.

Shults, LeRon and Steven Sandage. *Transforming Spirituality: Integrating Theology and Psychology*. Grand Rapids, Mich.: Baker, 2006.

Chapter 2: Friendship with God

Augustine. *Confessions*, trans. R. S. Pine-Coffin. London: Penguin, 1961.

Bernard of Clairvaux. *On Loving God*. In *Selected Works*, 173–205, trans. G. R. Evans. New York and Mahwah, N.J.: Paulist Press, 1987.

Brother Lawrence. *The Practice of the Presence of God*, trans. John Delaney. New York: Doubleday, 1977.

Houston, James. *The Transforming Power of Prayer: Deepening Your Friendship with God*. Colorado Springs: NavPress, 1996.

Humphrey, Edith. *Ecstasy and Intimacy: When the Holy Spirit Meets the Human Spirit*. Grand Rapids, Mich.: Eerdmans, 2006.

Packer, J. I. *Knowing God*. Downers Grove, Ill.: InterVarsity Press, 1973.

Piper, John. *Desiring God*. Sisters, Ore.: Multnomah, 2003.

Tozer, A. W. *The Knowledge of the Holy*. San Francisco: Harper and Row, 1961.

_____. *The Pursuit of God*. Harrisburg, Pa.: Christian Publications, 1948.

Willard, Dallas. *Hearing God*. Downers Grove, Ill.: InterVarsity Press, 1999.

CHAPTER 3: EXPERIENCING COMMUNITY

Benedict of Nursia. *The Rule of St. Benedict*, trans. Abbot Parry. Leominster, England: Gracewing, 1990.

Benner, David. *Sacred Companions: The Gift of Spiritual Friendship and Direction.* Downers Grove, Ill.: InterVarsity Press, 2002.

Bonhoeffer, Dietrich. *Life Together.* San Francisco: Harper and Row, 1954.

Scazzero, Peter. *The Emotionally Healthy Church.* Grand Rapids, Mich.: Zondervan, 2003.

Volf, Miroslav. *Exclusion and Embrace.* Nashville: Abingdon, 1996.

_____. *Free of Charge: Giving and Forgiving in a Culture Stripped of Grace.* Grand Rapids, Mich.: Zondervan, 2005.

Webster, Douglas. *Soulcraft: How God Shapes Us through Relationships.* Downers Grove, Ill.: InterVarsity Press, 1999.

CHAPTER 4: THE RENEWAL OF HOLINESS

Gill, David. *Becoming Good.* Downers Grove, Ill.: InterVarsity Press, 2000.

Gregory of Nyssa. *Life of Moses*, trans. Abraham Malherbe and Everett Ferguson. New York: Paulist Press, 1978.

Packer, J. I. *Keep in Step with the Spirit.* Old Tappan, N.J.: Revell, 1984.

_____. *Rediscovering Holiness.* Ann Arbor, Mich.: Servant, 1992.

Smith, Hannah Whitall. *The Christian's Secret of a Happy Life.* Westwood, N.J.: Revell, 1957.

Sproul, R. C. *The Holiness of God.* Wheaton, Ill.: Tyndale, 1985.

Thomas à Kempis. *The Imitation of Christ*, trans. E. M. Blaiklock. London: Hodder and Stoughton, 1979.

Willard, Dallas. *Renovation of the Heart.* Colorado Springs: NavPress, 2002.

CHAPTER 5: THE HEALING OF OUR WOUNDS

Anderson, Ray. *Self Care: A Theology of Personal Empowerment and Spiritual Healing.* Wheaton, Ill.: Bridgepoint, 1995.

Athanasius. *Life of Antony and the Letter to Marcellinus*, trans. Robert Gregg. New York: Paulist Press, 1980.

Benner, David. *The Gift of Being Yourself.* Downers Grove, Ill.: InterVarsity Press, 2004.

_____. *Healing Emotional Wounds.* Grand Rapids, Mich.: Baker, 1990.

Kidd, Sue Monk. *When the Heart Waits.* San Francisco: HarperSanFrancisco, 1992.

Nouwen, Henri. *Wounded Healer.* New York: Image, 1972.

Seamands, David. *Healing Grace.* Wheaton, Ill.: Victor, 1988.

Smedes, Lewis. *Shame and Grace: Healing the Shame We Don't Deserve.* San Francisco: HarperSan Francisco, 1993.

CHAPTER 6: DISCOVERING PURPOSE AND MEANING

Augustine. *The City of God*, trans. Henry Bettenson. London: Penguin, 1972.

Bockmuehl, Klaus. *Living by the Gospel*. Colorado Springs: Helmers and Howard, 1986.

Bonhoeffer, Dietrich. *The Cost of Discipleship*, trans. R. H. Fuller. London: SCM, 1959.

Bunyan, John. *The Pilgrim's Progress*. New York: Signet, 1964.

Merton, Thomas. *The Seven Storey Mountain: An Autobiography of Faith*. San Diego: Harcourt Brace, 1998.

Nouwen, Henri. *The Return of the Prodigal Son*. New York: Doubleday, 1992.

Warren, Rick. *The Purpose Driven® Life*. Grand Rapids, Mich.: Zondervan, 2002.

Willard, Dallas. *The Divine Conspiracy*. San Francisco: HarperSanFrancisco, 1998.

CHAPTER 7: THE GIFT OF A PERSONAL CALLING

Hardy, Lee. *The Fabric of This World*. Grand Rapids, Mich.: Eerdmans, 1990.

Ignatius of Loyola. *Spiritual Exercises and Selected Works*, ed. George Ganss. New York and Mahwah, N.J.: Paulist Press, 1991.

Palmer, Parker. *The Active Life: A Spirituality of Work, Creativity, and Caring*. San Francisco: Jossey-Bass, 1990.

_____. *Let Your Life Speak: Listening for the Voice of Vocation*. San Francisco: Jossey-Bass, 2000.

Smith, Gordon. *Courage and Calling*. Downers Grove, Ill.: InterVarsity Press, 2000.

_____. *Listening to God in Times of Choice*. Downers Grove, Ill.: InterVarsity Press, 1997.

_____. *The Voice of Jesus*. Downers Grove, Ill.: InterVarsity Press, 2003.

CHAPTER 8: AN INTEGRATED SPIRITUALITY

Foster, Richard. *Prayer*. San Francisco: HarperSan Francisco, 1992.

_____. *Streams of Living Water: Celebrating the Great Traditions of Christian Faith*. San Francisco: HarperSan Francisco, 1998.

Foster, Richard and James Smith, eds. *Devotional Classics*. San Francisco: Harper San Francisco, 1993.

Hollinger, Dennis. *Head, Heart, and Hands: Bringing Together Christian Thought, Passion, and Action*. Downers Grove, Ill.: InterVarsity Press, 2005.

Merton, Thomas. *New Seeds of Contemplation*. Norfolk, Conn.: New Directions, 1972.

_____. *No Man Is an Island*. San Diego: Harcourt, 1955.

Mulholland, Robert, Jr. *Invitation to a Journey: A Road Map for Spiritual Formation*. Downers Grove, Ill.: InterVarsity Press, 2003.

Nouwen, Henri. *Reaching Out: The Three Movements of the Spiritual Life*. New York: Doubleday, 1975.

Taylor, Howard and Geraldine Taylor. *Hudson Taylor's Spiritual Secret*. London: China Inland Mission, 1932.

CHAPTER 9: LIVING WITH DISCIPLINED INTENT

Dawn, Marva. *Keeping the Sabbath Wholly*. Grand Rapids, Mich.: Eerdmans, 1989.

De Sales, Francis. *Introduction to the Devout Life*, trans. J. K. Ryan. Garden City, N.Y.: Image, 1972.

Foster, Richard. *Celebration of Discipline*, rev. ed. San Francisco: HarperSan Francisco, 1988.

Griffin, Emilie. *Wilderness Time: A Guide to Spiritual Retreat*. San Francisco: Harper San Francisco, 1997.

Norris, Kathleen. *The Cloister Walk*. New York: Riverhead, 1996.

Peterson, Eugene. *Eat This Book: A Conversation in the Art of Spiritual Reading*. Grand Rapids, Mich.: Eerdmans, 2005.

Thompson, Marjorie. *Soul Feast: An Invitation to the Christian Spiritual Life*. Louisville, Ky.: Westminster John Knox, 1995.

Wesley, John and Charles Wesley. *Selected Prayers, Hymns, Journal Notes, Sermons, Letters, and Treatises*, ed. Frank Whaling. New York: Paulist Press, 1981.

Whitney, Donald. *Spiritual Disciplines for the Christian Life*. Colorado Springs: NavPress, 1991.

Willard, Dallas. *The Spirit of the Disciplines*. San Francisco: Harper and Row, 1988.

EPILOGUE: YEARNING FOR BETTER DAYS

Clapp, Rodney. *Tortured Wonders*. Grand Rapids, Mich.: Brazos, 2004.

Green, Thomas. *When the Well Runs Dry*. Notre Dame, Ind.: Ave Maria Press, 1979.

John of the Cross. *The Dark Night*. In *Selected Writings*, 157–209, ed. Kieran Kavanaugh. New York: Paulist Press, 1984.

Lamott, Anne. *Traveling Mercies*. New York: Pantheon, 1999 (paperback ed., New York: Anchor 2000).

Yaconelli, Mike. *Messy Spirituality*. Grand Rapids, Mich.: Zondervan, 2003.

NOTES

PROLOGUE: SLEEPING THROUGH A. W. TOZER'S LAST SERMON

1. In his book *The Smell of Sawdust* (Grand Rapids, Mich.: Zondervan, 2000), Richard Mouw reminds us that we should treasure aspects of a heritage like that.

INTRODUCTION : TWO SAINTS UNDER ONE HOOD

1. John Coffey, "Samuel Rutherford (1600–61): The Man behind the Myth," *St. Mary's College Bulletin*, no. 40 (Spring 1998): 55.
2. There is Henri Nouwen's vision in *Reaching Out* (New York: Doubleday, 1975) of the three movements of the spiritual life: to our innermost self, to our fellow human beings, and to our God; the organization of Richard Foster's book in *Prayer* (San Francisco: HarperSan Francisco, 1992) into three movements: inward in pursuit of transformation, upward in search of intimacy with God, and outward in search of ministry; and most recently, David Benner's insight in *The Gift of Being Yourself* (Downers Grove, Ill.: InterVarsity Press, 2004) that the spiritual journey involves relationship, transformation, and obedience.
3. "Spirituality that's not theological will grope in the darkness, and theology that's not spiritual will be emptied of its most important content" (Miroslav Volf, *Free of Charge* [Grand Rapids, Mich.: Zondervan, 2005], 236).

CHAPTER 1: GETTING STARTED

1. Richard Lovelace, "Evangelical Spirituality: A Church Historian's Perspective," in *Exploring Christian Spirituality*, ed. Kenneth Collins (Grand Rapids, Mich.: Baker, 2000), 225.
2. Gordon Fee, *Listening to the Spirit in the Text* (Grand Rapids, Mich.: Eerdmans, 2000), 4.
3. Edith Humphrey, *Intimacy and Ecstasy* (Grand Rapids, Mich.: Eerdmans, 2005), 5.
4. Evelyn Underhill, *The Spiritual Life* (Oxford, England: Oneworld, 1993), 27.
5. Fee, *Listening to the Spirit*, ch. 4.
6. Thomas Cahill, *How the Irish Saved Civilization* (New York: Doubleday, 1995), 218.
7. Cited by Huston Smith, *The World's Religions* (San Francisco: HarperSanFrancisco, 1991), 281.
8. Martin Buber, *I and Thou*, 2nd ed., trans. Ronald Smith (New York: Charles Scribner's Sons, 1958), 11.

9. Ralph Wood, "Outward Faith, Inward Piety: The Dependence of Spirituality on Worship and Doctrine," in *For All the Saints: Evangelical Theology and Christian Spirituality*, ed. Timothy George and Alister McGrath (Louisville, Ky.: Westminster John Knox, 2003), 95.

10. James Houston, *The Transforming Power of Prayer* (Colorado Springs: NavPress, 1996); originally published as *The Transforming Friendship* (1989).

11. Thomas Smail, *Reflected Glory: The Spirit in Christ and Christians* (Grand Rapids, Mich.: Eerdmans, 1976).

CHAPTER 2: FRIENDSHIP WITH GOD

1. Glen G. Scorgie, "Yearning for God: The Potential and Poverty of the Catholic Spirituality of Francis de Sales," *Journal of the Evangelical Theological Society* 41, no. 3 (Sept. 1998): 439–53.

2. M. de la Bedoyere, *Francois de Sales* (New York: Harper, 1960), 10.

3. Quoted by Wendy Wright, "Francois de Sales: Gentleness and Civility," in *Roots of the Modern Christian Tradition*, ed. E. R. Elder (Kalamazoo, Mich.: Cistercian, 1984), 133.

4. Wendy Wright and Joseph Power, introduction to *Francis de Sales, Jane de Chantel: Letters of Spiritual Direction* (New York and Mahwah, N.J.: Paulist Press, 1988), 30.

5. A. W. Tozer, *Knowledge of the Holy* (San Francisco: Harper and Row, 1961), 9.

6. James Houston, *The Transforming Power of Prayer* (Colorado Springs: NavPress, 1996), 10.

7. Ellen Charry, *By the Renewing of Your Minds* (New York and Oxford: Oxford University Press, 1997), 227.

8. Basil Pennington, quoted by David Benner, *The Gift of Being Yourself* (Downers Grove, Ill.: InterVarsity Press, 2004), 11.

9. Arthur Cochrane, ed., *Reformed Confessions of the Sixteenth Century* (Louisville, Ky.: Westminster John Knox, 2003), 305.

10. Emily Dickinson, "It Was Too Late for Man" (ca. 1862); available from www.bartleby.com/113; accessed 11 July 2006.

11. Henri Nouwen, *Reaching Out* (New York: Doubleday, 1975), 21–62.

CHAPTER 3: EXPERIENCING COMMUNITY

1. Compare Thomas Merton, *No Man Is an Island* (San Diego: Harcourt, 1955).

2. Thus James Houston writes: "If we find it hard to form lasting relationships with those we see around us, then we will find it very hard to relate in any depth to the God we cannot see" (*The Transforming Power of Prayer* [Colorado Springs: NavPress, 1996], 21–22).

3. Walter Rauschenbusch, *A Theology of the Social Gospel* (New York and Nashville: Abingdon, 1917), 108.

4. Ibid., 97, 109.

5. Miroslav Volf, *Exclusion and Embrace* (Nashville: Abingdon, 1996), 29; Volf, "Exclusion and Embrace," in *Emerging Voices in Global Christian Theology*, ed. W. Dryness (Grand Rapids, Mich.: Zondervan, 1994), 27, 39.

6. Myrla Siebold, "When the Wounding Runs Deep: Encouragement for Those on the Road to Forgiveness," in *Care of the Soul*, ed. Mark McMinn and Timothy Phillips (Downers Grove, Ill.: InterVarsity Press, 2001), 294–308.

7. David Benner, *Sacred Companions: The Gift of Spiritual Friendship and Direction* (Downers Grove, Ill.: InterVarsity Press, 2002), 17.

8. Based on interaction with Avery Dulles, *Models of the Church*, exp. ed. (New York: Doubleday, 1987), esp. chs. 4–5.

9. C. S. Lewis, *The Abolition of Man* (New York: Macmillan, 1947), 80.

10. Avery Dulles, *Testimonial to Grace* (New York: Sheed and Ward, 1946), 50–54.

CHAPTER 4: THE RENEWAL OF HOLINESS

1. John Wesley's legacy includes an often revised publication entitled *A Plain Account of Christian Perfection* (1777).

2. Adapted from Walker Percy, *Lost in the Cosmos* (New York: Farrar, Straus and Giroux, 1983), 57–69.

3. As quoted in Michael Ford, *Wounded Prophet: A Portrait of Henri J. M. Nouwen* (New York: Doubleday, 1999), 213.

4. Eugene Peterson, *Answering God: The Psalms as Tools for Prayer* (New York: Harper and Row, 1989), ch. 8.

5. *Character* is a person's moral nature or fixed moral disposition; *virtue* is a positive or ideal quality of character that has been learned or acquired.

6. Martin Luther, *Commentary on St. Paul's Epistle to the Galatians* (Westwood, N.J.: Revell, 1953), 157.

CHAPTER 5: THE HEALING OF OUR WOUNDS

1. We must also be discerning of those occasional situations where the Evil One appears to be the direct cause of the suffering, and accordingly needs to be addressed with spiritual authority.

2. Quoted by Anne Lamott, *Traveling Mercies*, paperback ed. (New York: Anchor, 2000), 112.

3. Francis Schaeffer, *True Spirituality* (Wheaton, Ill.: Tyndale, 1971), 134–47.

4. *Dictionary of Pentecostal and Charismatic Movements*, ed. Stanley Burgess and Gary McGee (Grand Rapids, Mich.: Zondervan, 1988), under "Healing Movements," 373.

5. Athanasius, *Life of Antony and the Letter to Marcellinus*, trans. Robert Gregg (New York: Paulist Press, 1980), 74.

6. Richard Foster, *Streams of Living Water* (San Francisco: HarperSan Francisco, 1998), 30.

7. Athanasius, *Life of Antony*, 74.
8. Foster, *Streams of Living Water*, 30.
9. Athanasius, *Life of Antony*, 94.
10. Mike Flynn and Doug Gregg, *Inner Healing* (Downers Grove, Ill.: InterVarsity Press, 1993), esp. ch. 3.
11. Thomas Merton, *No Man Is an Island* (San Diego: Harcourt, 1955), ix–x.
12. David Benner, *The Gift of Being Yourself* (Downers Grove, Ill.: InterVarsity Press, 2004), esp. ch. 3 and p. 110.
13. Henri Nouwen, *Wounded Healer* (New York: Image, 1972).

CHAPTER 6: DISCOVERING PURPOSE AND MEANING

1. Augustine, *The City of God*, 12.1.
2. Ibid., 18.1.
3. Klaus Bockmuehl, *Living by the Gospel: Christian Roots of Confidence and Purpose* (Colorado Springs: Helmers and Howard, 1986).
4. Margaret Silf, *Inner Compass: An Invitation to Ignatian Spirituality* (Chicago: Loyola University Press, 1999), xix.
5. Albert Camus, *The Myth of Sisyphus, and Other Essays*, trans. Justin O'Brien (New York: Vintage, 1955), 119–23.
6. Viktor Frankl, *Man's Search for Meaning*, 3rd ed. (New York: Simon and Schuster, 1984), 84.
7. William Willimon, *Clergy and Laity Burnout* (Nashville: Abingdon, 1989), 50.
8. Bockmuehl, *Living by the Gospel*, 32.
9. Ellen Charry, *By the Renewing of Your Minds* (New York and Oxford: Oxford University Press, 1997), 233.
10. Hilary of Poitiers, *De Trinitate*, 1:37–38; quoted in *Early Christian Prayers*, ed. A. Hamman, trans. Walter Mitchell (Chicago: Henry Regnery; London: Longmans, Green, 1961), 194.
11. Aaron Smith, "Participation in the Divine Disposition: The Nature of the Knowledge of God" (M.Div. thesis, Bethel Seminary San Diego, 2003).

CHAPTER 7: THE GIFT OF A PERSONAL CALLING

1. Irene Mahoney, intro. to *Marie of the Incarnation: Selected Writings* (New York: Paulist Press, 1989), 5–40.
2. Ibid., 2.
3. Suzanne Farnham et al., *Listening Hearts* (Harrisburg, Pa.: Morehouse, 1991), 115, n. 13.
4. Frederick Buechner, *Wishful Thinking: A Seeker's ABC*, rev. ed. (San Francisco: HarperSan Francisco, 1993), 119.
5. Ibid., 118–19.

6. Vocation is found in "genuine service to others through the responsible use of our talents and abilities" (Lee Hardy, *The Fabric of This World* [Grand Rapids, Mich.: Eerdmans, 1990], xvii).

7. This is suggested by Debra Rienstra, *So Much More* (San Francisco: Jossey-Bass, 2005), 220.

8. Søren Kierkegaard, *Fear and Trembling/Repetition*, trans. Howard Hong and Edna Hong (Princeton, N.J.: Princeton University Press, 1983), 1–123.

9. John Stott, *The Sermon on the Mount* (Downers Grove, Ill.: InterVarsity Press, 1978), 49.

10. Miroslav Volf, *Exclusion and Embrace* (Nashville: Abingdon, 1996), ch. 6.

11. Dallas Willard, *Hearing God* (Downers Grove, Ill.: InterVarsity Press, 1999), 182.

12. Francis de Sales, *Introduction to the Devout Life*, trans. J. K. Ryan (Garden City, N.Y.: Image, 1972), 39–43.

13. Compare Willard, *Hearing God*, ch. 8 on recognizable qualities of God's voice.

14. Ted Peters, *Sin: Radical Evil in Soul and Society* (Grand Rapids, Mich.: Eerdmans, 1994), esp. ch. 2.

15. Quoted by Robert Johnston, *Reel Spirituality* (Grand Rapids, Mich.: Baker, 2000), 151.

16. See esp. Gordon Smith, *Courage and Calling* (Downers Grove, Ill.: InterVarsity Press, 2000).

CHAPTER 8: AN INTEGRATED SPIRITUALITY

1. Available from http://www.lonniefrisbee.com/whowas.htm; accessed 3 November 2005.

2. *Frisbee: The Life and Death of a Hippie Preacher*, dir. David Di Sabatino, documentary motion picture, 2005.

3. Gordon Smith, *The Voice of Jesus* (Downers Grove, Ill.: InterVarsity Press, 2003), 74.

4. William May, "The Virtues in a Professional Setting," in *Readings in Christian Ethics*, vol. 1, ed. David Clark and Robert Rakestraw (Grand Rapids, Mich.: Baker, 1994), 270.

5. Lee Hardy, *The Fabric of This World* (Grand Rapids, Mich.: Eerdmans, 1990), 54–63.

6. John Calvin, *Commentary on a Harmony of the Evangelists*, trans. William Pringle, 3 vols. (Grand Rapids, Mich.: Eerdmans, 1949), vol. 2, 143.

7. Hardy, *Fabric of This World*, 57.

8. Richard Foster, *Prayer* (San Francisco: HarperSan Francisco, 1992).

9. It's what Frederick Buechner had in mind, I suspect, when he suggested that sometimes we are more religious than God is.

10. John Webster Grant, *Moon of Wintertime* (Toronto: University of Toronto Press, 1984), 115.

11. Quoted in Chris De Vinck, ed., *Nouwen Then* (Grand Rapids, Mich.: Zondervan, 1999), 33.

12. Carl F. H. Henry, "Spiritual? Say It Isn't So!" in *Alive to God: Studies in Spirituality*, ed. J. I. Packer and Loren Wilkinson (Downers Grove, Ill.: InterVarsity Press, 1992), 13.

CHAPTER 9: LIVING WITH DISCIPLINED INTENT

1. Thomas Alan Harvey, *Acquainted with Grief: Wang Mingdao's Stand for the Persecuted Church in China* (Grand Rapids, Mich.: Brazos, 2002).

2. Quoted by Alister McGrath, "Loving God with Heart and Mind: The Theological Foundations of Spirituality," in *For All the Saints: Evangelical Theology and Christian Spirituality*, ed. Timothy George and Alister McGrath (Louisville, Ky.: Westminster John Knox, 2003), 11–12.

3. Ignatius of Loyola, *The Spiritual Exercises and Selected Works*, ed. George Ganss (New York and Mahwah, N.J.: Paulist Press, 1991), 121.

4. Gordon Fee, *Listening to the Spirit in the Text* (Grand Rapids, Mich.: Eerdmans, 2000), 37.

5. Timothy George suggests that evangelical spirituality can be revitalized by recoupling justification by faith and union with Christ, in *For All the Saints*, ed. George and McGrath, 4.

6. Dallas Willard, *Hearing God* (Downers Grove, Ill.: InterVarsity Press, 1999), 194.

7. Don Postema, *Space for God*, 2nd ed. (Grand Rapids, Mich.: Christian Reformed Church, 1996).

8. Marva Dawn, *Keeping the Sabbath Wholly* (Grand Rapids, Mich.: Eerdmans, 1989); Klaus Issler, *Wasting Time with God* (Downers Grove, Ill.: InterVarsity Press, 2001).

9. Glen Scorgie, "Hermeneutics and the Meditative Use of Scripture: The Case for a Baptized Imagination," *Journal of the Evangelical Theological Society* 44, no. 2 (June 2001): 271–84.

10. Dietrich Bonhoeffer, *Life Together* (San Francisco: Harper and Row, 1954), 83, 89.

11. Macrina Wiederkehr, quoted by Marjorie Thompson, *Soul Feast* (Louisville, Ky.: Westminster John Knox, 1995), 18.

12. Quoted by Simon Chan, *Spiritual Theology* (Downers Grove, Ill.: InterVarsity Press, 1998), 170–71.

13. Mary Lathbury and Alexander Groves, "Break Thou the Bread of Life," *Hymns of the Christian Life* (Camp Hill, Pa.: Christian Publications, 1978), 411.

14. David Benner, *Sacred Companions: The Gift of Spiritual Friendship and Direction* (Downers Grove, Ill.: InterVarsity Press, 2002), 15.

15. Augustine, *Sermons* 115.4.4; quoted in *New Westminster Dictionary of Christian Spirituality*, ed. Philip Sheldrake (Louisville, Ky.: Westminster John Knox, 2005), under "Augustinian Spirituality."

16. Ibid.

17. Thompson, *Soul Feast*, ch. 9.

EPILOGUE: YEARNING FOR BETTER DAYS

1. Yet even in the best of times "an unattainable ecstasy has hovered just beyond the grasp of [our] consciousness" (C. S. Lewis, *The Problem of Pain* [London: Collins, 1957], 136).

2. Adapted from John Magee, "High Flyer" (1941); available from www.qunl.com/rees0008.html; accessed 28 July 2006.

3. Martin Luther, *Luther's Larger Catechism*, trans. J. N. Lenker (Minneapolis: Augsburg, 1967), 104–106.

4. John Bunyan, *The Pilgrim's Progress* (New York: Signet, 1964), 18–19.

We want to hear from you. Please send your comments about this book to us in care of zreview@zondervan.com. Thank you.

ZONDERVAN.com/
AUTHORTRACKER
follow your favorite authors